God, my Girlfriends and Me

God, my Girlfriends and Me

Nurturing the Three Most Important Relationships in a Woman's Life

MARCIA RAMIREZ

GAMG PUBLISHING HOUSE
Nashville, Tennessee

GOD, MY GIRLFRIENDS AND ME
Nurturing the Three Most Important Relationships in a Woman's Life
Copyright © 2022 by Marcia Ramirez.
All rights reserved.

No portion of this book, except for brief review, may be reproduced, stored in a retrieval system, or transmitted in any form or by any means—electronic, mechanical, photocopying, recording, or otherwise without the written permission of the author.

FIRST EDITION
Published by GAMG Publishing House
P.O. BOX 140732, Nashville, TN 37214

Cover design and formatting: Mary Sue Englund
Marcia Ramirez photo: John Albani
Edited by: Emily Wells

Issued in print, electronic and audio formats.
ISBN 979-8-218-02613-4

For information, contact
Marcia Ramirez at gamgministries@gmail.com
or via her website: www.marciaramirez.com

*For Charlotte, and all the other girls out there:
May you always know your inherent worth,
be surrounded by good friends,
and never doubt God's incredible love for you.*

Table of Contents

Prologue 7
Introduction 11
My Story 19

Part One: *YOU: Where It Begins*

1. What do I think about myself? 33
2. Self-care 45
3. Limits 55
4. Seasons 67
5. Your story matters 81

Part Two: *GIRLFRIENDS: We Were Made For Community*

6. What do I think about my friends? 97
7. Friendship Killers 107
8. Why Diversity Matters 127
9. Iron Sharpens Iron 145
10. Friendship in the Bible 155

Part Three: *GOD: The Great Connection*

11. What do I think about God? 169
12. Soul Care 177
13. Abba's Child 187
14. Evolving Faith 197
15. Rooted In The Eternal 207

Epilogue 213
Acknowledgements 217
notes 221

Prologue

"*MARCIA, WHERE ARE YOU? Have you got a minute to talk?*" As soon as I saw the text on my phone, I knew my friend was in trouble. "*Of course, honey. I'm at home. Call me anytime.*" Her number immediately appeared on the screen and I answered, trying to sound upbeat and normal, like I wasn't expecting a problem. "*Hey Laura, what's up girl?*" At first, I heard only silence, so I said, "*Laura? Are you there? Are you ok?*" It was at that point I heard the quiet sobs on the other end of the line, confirming my initial gut reaction. "*Oh friend,*" I said. "*Take your time. Cry it out. Then tell me what's wrong when you can. I'm here and I'll wait as long as you need me to.*" Of course, my mind was immediately racing to worst case scenarios. Had someone died? Did her husband just ask her for a divorce? Had someone in her family just gotten a cancer diagnosis? What could it be?

Laura and I had been friends for years, but I realized in that moment that it had been quite a while since she and I had really talked. I felt a little embarrassed to admit that I wasn't really sure what recent developments could be going on in her life. After a little bit more silence and crying, she finally blurted out just four words. "*I'm . . . just . . . so . . . tired.*"

Hmmmmm . . . I didn't quite know how to respond. She's tired?? I mean, most women I know these days are tired, running on fumes and adrenaline just to get through each day. There had to be more to the story. "*What do you mean, exactly?*" I gently asked. "*Do you think you need to see a doctor?*" I heard her sigh deeply and then she said, "*I don't know. Maybe. All I know is that I can't go on like this for one more day.*" It was at that moment I said, "*I'm getting in my car right now. I'll be at your house in 10 mins. DON'T GO ANYWHERE.*"

When she opened the door to her home, I could tell she was beyond "tired." She was spent. Exhausted in every way—physically, emotionally, mentally, and spiritually. How did she get this way? And how, as her friend, did I not see the signs before now? Sadly, there are too many "Lauras" out there, juggling careers and families and many other social commitments—to the point that they find themselves utterly falling apart from exhaustion. Human beings aren't made to give and give and give without taking time to refuel themselves. They will always crash and burn. My friend was in "crash and burn" mode right before my eyes. How did I know? Because I've been there myself —-wayyyyyy too many times.

Prologue

* * *

I was married with a child by the time I was 21, so all the responsibilities of being a wife and mother came early in my life. I did my best, but I failed often, adding the weight of guilt onto my already burdened, people-pleasing shoulders. I spent my days trying to figure out who I needed to be to make those around me happy and forgot that my own happiness needed to be figured into the equation.

For years I struggled because I didn't know how to develop authentic and healthy relationships. I spent most days feeling deeply lonely, even though I was rarely alone. I didn't really believe I deserved to be loved just for who I was—so I lived my life over-committed, over-worked, and un-done, hoping that I could somehow earn the love I was craving. I even used that approach with God. (If I did everything that my religion taught me to do— maybe even a few extra things!—I might earn God's love). Newsflash—it didn't work! Actually, none of my "works" won me the love I was craving. I also made a lot of bad choices in my younger days, trying to be the perfect wife, mother, friend, daughter, co-worker etc. and all I did was lose myself in that whole mess. I was miserable, lonely and exhausted. Believe me, I had several "crash and burn" moments . . . until one day, I had enough.

I've often heard that the definition of crazy is "doing the same thing over and over, expecting different results." I was tired of the repeating patterns, always leaving me in the same place—unhappy, lonely, and afraid. I knew that the only person who could truly change my life, my circumstances, my *story* was me. I knew deep down that at the core of all my problems was my inability to develop and rest in loving, authentic relationships . . . with God, with others, and with myself.

My life didn't change overnight, but little by little I started making significant changes that have helped me to create a life full of joy, peace, contentment, and love. A life anchored by an authentic spirituality, good friends, and healthier sense of self. A life I actually *want* to live. I want to help you do the same.

Have you ever found yourself facing "crash and burn" mode? Maybe you are there right now. Maybe you are desperate for some relief and that's why you picked up this book.

Girlfriend, hang on. You have come to the right place. Help is on the way.

Love,

Marcia

INTRODUCTION

The Big Three

I'VE HEARD IT SAID that women are born nurturers. It's as if God created us that way for a reason and most of us find that it comes naturally to us. However, when I look around, it's clear that most of the women I know run themselves ragged, nurturing everyone and everything around them, and overlooking the most important relationships that they desperately need to nurture. I call them "The Big Three": God, your girlfriends, and you.

How we see and relate to God, our friends and ourselves will dictate all the other relationships in our lives and will determine how affective we are in them.

It's all about learning how to love.

And we do that by elevating and prioritizing The Big Three "VIRs"—*Very Important Relationships.*

God and My Girlfriends

In Matthew 22, one of the Pharisees (the religious scholars of biblical times) posed this question to Jesus: "*Teacher, which commandment in the law is the greatest?*" Jesus answered him by saying,

> *"Love the Lord your God with all your heart and with all your soul and with all your mind. This is the first and greatest commandment. And the second is like it: Love your neighbor as yourself. All the Law and the Prophets hang on these two commandments."* [1]

Let's break that down, shall we? Jesus says there are three relationships we are to nurture and prioritize:

1. Our relationship with **God.** We are to love him with all our heart, soul and mind.

2. Our relationship with our **neighbor.** We are to love our neighbor as much and *as well as* we love ourselves. Who is our "neighbor"? That would be anyone really . . . family, friends, acquaintances, co-workers, even strangers. Our neighbors are just "others."

Which leads us to our third "VIR", and the one that many of us completely ignore:

The Big Three

3. Our relationship with **ourselves**. I mean, when Jesus says, "Love your neighbor *as yourself*" then obviously we must learn to love ourselves well in order to love our neighbors in the same way, right?

One of my favorite translations of that verse in Matthew 22 is from The Passion translation. It says:

"Love the Lord your God with every passion of your heart, with all the energy of your being, and with every thought that is within you." And then it says, **"And you must love your friend in the same way you love yourself."**

Jesus made it very clear—it's all about love. Loving God well, loving each other well, and yes, loving ourselves well.

* * *

In **Part One** of this book, we will focus on how to love ourselves in a healthy way. It may seem that loving ourselves would be easy, but it's the back-half of that sentence that people struggle with—*in a healthy way.*

Many religious teachers have tried to tell us that we should "deny ourselves"—even "hate ourselves." They pull scripture out of context to try and back up their teachings. But the more I dig into my Bible and study the scriptures, the more I believe this is bad theology. We are made in God's image, so why would we want to "deny" that? And we certainly shouldn't hate it!

God and My Girlfriends

Franciscan friar and spiritual author, Father Richard Rohr breaks down "self" into two parts: The false self and the true self. The false self is ego driven. We cannot allow the false self to control or dictate our hearts—or our way of thinking. Instead, we need to nurture our true self. This is the key to a healthy, happy life that is connected to God.

What is our true self? Some definitions describe it as: "the most authentic version of you," "the purest part of yourself"[2], "what religion often calls the soul"[3]. I believe that our true self in its purest form is . . . love. The love that's placed inside of us by our Creator. Getting in touch with that love and letting it lead us in all our relationships is what Jesus had in mind when he said, "All the law hangs on these commandments." Nothing we do really matters if we aren't doing it with love. Finding our true self is how we can grow into beautiful vessels of God's love in the world and avoid being "clanging cymbals." [4]

In **Part Two**, we will dive into nurturing our friendships. I talk to so many women who feel that they have been let down over and over again by their friends. Because of that hurt, they sometimes isolate and become filled with distrust. This is one of the reasons why loneliness has reached epidemic proportions in our world today. It is critical for our overall health to have healthy friendships in our lives.

Have you ever heard the phrase, "Show me your friends and I'll show you your future"? Finding and keeping great

The Big Three

friends is likely to be one of the most important skills you can develop in life. Proverbs 13:20 says, *"Spend time with the wise and you will become wise."* Jesus was friends with everyone, but he picked his closest circle very carefully. The people you choose to surround yourself with will be the strongest influences in your life. They will either make you wiser or more foolish. However, choosing good friends is just part of the equation. It's equally important to learn how to *be* a good friend. To attract wise friends, we must commit to being a wise friend as well.

Finally, in **Part Three**, we will cover the most important relationship of all: our relationship with God, our Creator. You will notice that in my writings I have chosen to use the pronoun "he" when I talk of God. I have learned in my more recent faith journey that many people struggle with referring to God as male. I get that. It says in the Bible that God is neither male nor female.[5] God is Spirit. God is Love. God is all encompassing and transcendent, well beyond gender labels. But, for many reasons, including the fact that the Bible refers to God as our "Heavenly Father" (male) and that Christians believe that God manifested himself in human form as a man, Jesus, the pro-noun "he" has been the common association. Ultimately, it's a connection with the spirit of God for which our souls yearn. Some of my spiritual friends choose to refer to and think of God in the feminine form, "she." Others prefer both male and female "they"— or even as just Spirit, "it". Use the pronoun that you are most comfortable with in order to feel connected to God. Without that healthy connection, we will wither on the vine. I hope my experiences will help guide you toward this life-giving relationship. It's truly what matters most.

* * *

You'll see in the pages of this book that I have been on a life-long journey towards learning how to love better in all my relationships. Mistakes I've made and lessons I've learned are all part of the process. And as I worked hard to improve my own life by getting these three relationships healthy, I started noticing that I wasn't alone.

The struggles I was having seemed to be common with many other women around me. . .and like my friend, Laura, were showing up in exhaustion of the body and soul.

That is why I decided to start God and My Girlfriends Ministries in 2018. It's a non-profit organization with the goal of helping us all learn to love and nurture those Big Three VIRs better. I want to give women the tools to put soul care, friendship care, and self-care back at the top of her priority list. I want to stop seeing women walk around exhausted from giving to everyone and everything except themselves. This book is part of that desire. Like I said, I have certainly been there myself, and truthfully, it still can be a daily struggle. But I hope that maybe some of the lessons from my own journey can be an encouragement for you.

The Big Three

For those that are married, and/or married with kids, it might be easy to feel conflicted about this message. Many of us have been programmed by our religions and/or cultures to always put being a wife and mother at the top of our priority list, sometimes to the detriment of our own sanity! I'm not saying we should shirk those responsibilities, but what I AM saying is that when we nurture the Big Three VIR's *first*, we will be better for everyone else too. We will be better wives, better mothers. Better co-workers, sisters, daughters, neighbors. We will just be BETTER— healthier and whole human beings.

So, pour yourself a cup of coffee, tea, wine, or whatever you love to sip on, and curl up in your favorite chair with this book today. Let's begin investing in these three relationships.

You are worth it.

Your friends are worth it.

Your soul is worth it.

My Story

EVERYONE HAS A STORY—and it is our story that shapes us and molds us into who we are. It is each person's unique combination of experiences, adventures, heartbreaks and joys that create our beliefs and opinions on just about everything. You'll read several parts of my story throughout this book, but I'd love to start by telling you a little bit about my upbringing.

I grew up in a small town: Arkadelphia, AR—population 10,123. That number is burned into my head from the many weekend nights I spent "cruising" from Arkadelphia to Caddo Valley and back during my high school days. You had to pass the population sign every time you'd make the route. I don't remember it *ever* changing as long as I lived there, which is kind of hilarious. I recently checked and the population as it stands today is 10,611, so apparently over the last 40 years it hasn't grown much, nor declined. Consistent is probably a good word for 'ol "Arkadoo," as the locals call it. A typical southern town with small town values.

Arkadelphia was a lovely place to grow up. Times were much simpler then. We felt safe leaving the doors of our homes and cars unlocked. Kids were allowed at a young age to play freely outside and walk around the town unaccompanied. You knew your banker, mailman and butcher by name. Most of the businesses were locally owned—very few "chains" in our little town back then. For me, it was a Mayberry-like experience, and I'm grateful for the sweet memories and beautiful friendships I cultivated there.

Now, that being said—as I have grown up, I have come to realize that there was a lot of darkness in that little town that I was sheltered from. I mean, it *was* the south in the 60's and 70's, so racism was even more outwardly prevalent than it is now. Lines were definitely drawn between the "black" part of town and the "white" part of town. There were race riots and threats of lynchings. I remember a cross being burned in the front yard of a white family because word had gotten out that their daughter was "hanging out with/dating" a black boy. It was a terrifying warning that the 2 races weren't supposed to intermingle. I also have a vivid memory of accidentally coming upon a KKK meeting when I was around 10 years old. I was spending the night with my friend Paula and we snuck out of the house in the middle of the night for some dumb-dumb reason that escapes me now. Anyway, Paula lived

My Story

out in the country and as we walked the woods behind her house, we heard men's voices. Of course we *had* to go find out what was going on.(Dumb-dumb move #2). The white robes and hoods are still burned into my memory. They were all gathered around a fire pit. Paula and I were both so sheltered from things like this that I remember her looking at me with wide eyes and quietly mouthing the words, "*Satan worshippers.*" Of course! That had to be it! We had been warned about Satan worshippers at church, but had never heard mention of a group of men that hated black people so much that they actually had secret meetings about how to control or even worse, get rid of them. I shudder when that memory pops up in my mind. No, things definitely weren't so innocent and simple in the lives of my black friends. I see that clearly now and it breaks my heart. Even though the population hasn't changed much there, I sure do pray that *that* has changed in Arkadelphia—as well as in every other small town in the south where racism was so cruel.

* * *

I was raised as an only child in a Christian home with loving parents. My Father was a college professor and my Mom was a "homemaker." In other words, she didn't work outside the home. I remember her dabbling in selling Tupperware, Avon, and then Amway, but she never really got any of those businesses off the ground. I think she just did it to try and keep herself busy and possibly bring in a little extra money. Dad loved his teaching job, but back then a small University professor didn't make a ton of money. They did manage their money well, so although we never had anything "extra," we never lacked for any necessities either. For instance, I may have had to settle for off-brand clothes, order the cheapest thing on the menu in restaurants, and never buy anything that wasn't on sale or marked down, but I never had to worry about *having* clothes, or food in my belly. We were probably the pretty typical middle-class American family back then.

Mom, Dad and I were members of First Baptist Church while I was growing up. Both my parents taught Sunday School and Dad sometimes served as a deacon. I remember being there pretty much anytime the doors were open. Sunday morning, Sunday night, and Wednesday night services, along with choir practice, handbells and even GA's. For those of you reading this that aren't Baptists, GA's stands for "Girls In Action," which is a missions discipleship program for girls in grades 1–6. Yep, they start training us in missions early in the Southern Baptist world!

As I grew older, I got very involved in the FBC youth group. I loved hanging out at the "Youth House" with all my church friends. It was an older home that the church bought, and it sat directly across the street from the main church building. It was a place where the youth could have fellowship away from the prying eyes of parents. Of course we always had chaperones because no good Baptist parent would ever leave their teenagers unattended for too long. We might start DANCING for crying out

My Story

loud! *A little Baptist humor there. Sorry, couldn't help it. My roots are deep.

Being a member of FBC was a huge part of my life during my formative years. It was part of my original "order" of spirituality, which was so very necessary. And although I can say that my faith journey has evolved much from traditional Baptist beliefs, I know without a doubt that FBC Arkadelphia played a huge part in teaching me about Jesus in a way that has served me well through the years.

I was "saved," as the Baptists called it, at Camp Siloam, which is a summer church camp located in the NW Arkansas town of Siloam Springs. In my youth, I would always spend a week during the summers at Camp Siloam and I have very fond memories of my time there. Our days would be filled with hiking, swimming, learning campfire songs etc. . .all the typical camp activities you would expect at a youth camp. Of course, this was a Baptist camp, so along with the regular camp activities, we also had bible studies, missions training, and even sword drills. If you didn't grow up Southern Baptist, you might be asking "*What in the world is a 'sword drill*??" Well, the Bible is sometimes referred to as a "sword" in fundamental Christian circles, so a sword drill is a competitive exercise where several children or youth are lined up with their Bibles held out in front of them between their hands. Then the "driller" would call out a passage of a Bible verse and whoever found it in their bible first was the winner! Sounds super exciting, doesn't it? Don't ever say that we Southern

God and My Girlfriends

Baptists didn't know how to have a good time! Ha! (Side note, I was never good at sword drills and they made me a nervous wreck when I had to do them. I always walked away feeling like a loser and a bad Christian. So, if anyone else is squirming as you recall your days of sword drills, you aren't alone).

In the evenings at Camp Siloam, we would all gather under a covered pavilion for worship time together. After leading us in hymns, a pastor, counselor or guest speaker would take the stage to motivate and encourage us to turn our lives over to Jesus and "be saved". The summer of my 16th year, the message finally took. I walked down the aisle during the altar call (apparently moved by something the speaker of the evening had said) and tearfully told one of the camp counselors that I was ready to "give my life to Jesus". Of course, that was the goal at Camp Siloam—to either "save" you, or perhaps lead you into full-time ministry or missions. I'm sure my parents were thrilled that year to know their money was finally well-spent. I came home a full-fledged Christian! The next Sunday morning, in front of all our friends at First Baptist Arkadelphia, I was baptized, sealing the deal.

Of course, that "deal" has been tested many times since then. Many, many times! But I'm happy to report that our sweet Savior does indeed welcome back his prodigal son/daughter with open arms. . .over and over again. Jesus is the real deal, friends. This I know. But back to the story . . . After graduating from Arkadelphia High School, I was hon-

My Story

ored with a music scholarship to attend Ouachita Baptist University. I attended OBU for 2 years before switching to a different, but still religious-based, college for a short time, Harding University (I followed a boy. . .sigh . . . more about that later). Harding was a Church of Christ college and the year I attended was only the 2nd year that girls were allowed to wear pants on campus. It was a BIG DEAL. Before then, girls were only allowed to wear dresses. . .and I'm sure they were long dresses too. Was this the 1950's? Nope—1982. But this was a religious environment that was still holding on to deep patriarchy. At OBU, I thought the rules were strict—but they were nothin' compared to what I walked into at Harding.

I'm telling you about my childhood so you can understand how early religion started shaping my story and how important it was to my parents that I had a clear view of God. It was the culture I was born into and brought up in. I was "dedicated" to God by my parents and a little Bible was placed into my hands before I could even read or write. I was taught to pray before bedtime and before each meal. I practiced memorizing scripture and learned all the rules of how to be a good Christian girl. I was taught "right" from "wrong" and bought into the belief that to get to heaven I must act and behave in a certain way. I was loved and sheltered within the confines of our little Christian community, and I honestly didn't know people lived any other way.

What I have learned as an adult is that everyone's spiritual

God and My Girlfriends

journey is different and that's okay. That makes so much sense to me now. I say "now," because as you probably could glean from my childhood spiritual experiences, I thought everyone had to believe the exact same way, worship the exact same way, and interpret the Bible *the exact same way* in order to get to heaven. Catholics, Methodists, Lutherans, Presbyterians, Pentecostals, Anglicans, Episcopalians etc . . . were all out of luck! Clearly there was only one direct route into God's graces and that was the Southern Baptist way.

And then came the boy. I call him "the boy" because we truly were just kids when we fell in love, I got pregnant, and we got married—in that order. He was 19 and I was 20, and his religious affiliation was Church of Christ. Man, I thought the Southern Baptists were narrow in their religious views, but they were *little hellions* compared to the Church of Christ! At least that was my experience in the Church of Christ we attended in Arkansas. I now found myself in a church that was telling me that *their* way was the only path to heaven, NOT the Southern Baptist way. It was very confusing to me for quite awhile.

This new church even made me get re-baptized because, according to the minister there, I had *"only been baptized into the Baptist church, not God's church,"* so apparently my first baptism didn't count. That was news to me!

There were some lovely people in that church, but it was

My Story

legalistic in the harshest way. I always felt I was failing at being a Christian. I could never keep all the rules and never felt truly close to God. Unfortunately, I had no choice but to attend that church. My husband's family wouldn't approve of us going anywhere else, and pleasing the family was what we were taught to do. It was what we *wanted* to do.

Two years into our marriage we moved to Nashville, TN so he could pursue the music business. While his career quickly took off, our marriage suffered. There were many reasons, but those will remain private for now. However, the marriage definitely became a deeply toxic relationship and I walked away.

By age 29, I found myself a single Mom to a nine year old son, and my whole life was a mess. I had drifted far from any relationship with God because the rules just seemed too hard. I was truly living life with absolutely no rudder.

It wasn't long before I ended up in another bad marriage that was equally dysfunctional; I gave birth to another son, and then I got divorced . . . again. When I think back on those times, it truly breaks my heart. I was a MESS. But I can also see very clearly that, although I had turned away from God, he never turned away from me. He was working behind the scenes for his prodigal daughter to make sure she was protected. I couldn't see it at the time, but I sure see it now! God is good like that.

I was 34 years old before I finally realized that there was

more to Christianity than just following rules. I was at a rock-bottom moment when I ran into an old friend who invited me to a new church she had just started attending. That church and the people there became my lifeline back to God. They loved me as I was, yet with the desire to see me become a stronger, better version of myself. They wanted me to regain the strength and confidence that only comes from knowing that God's "got your back." Always. I had honestly forgotten that. This is just one of the many times that God used friends to help me find myself again. It's been a recurring theme in my life.

It wasn't overnight, but I slowly started finding freedom in Christ again. Freedom from the pain of rejection; freedom from the belief that I wasn't good enough; freedom from the guilt of my own actions that convinced me I could never be used for God's Kingdom. Man, if I had only paid more attention to the stories in the Bible, I would have seen that Jesus picked the broken-*est* of the broken to walk beside and join in community. What a relief. THANK YOU JESUS.

Over the last 20 years, I have found my peace, comfort and joy in the arms of my Savior again. And I finally found *healthy* love and stability with an amazing man, who has walked the road towards God with me. Together, we have grown closer to our Lord and have been very blessed to see how God provides for us without fail. Our kids are grown now, and we have settled into a new season of life. My prayer these days is that I get to help grow God and My

My Story

Girlfriends Ministries into a source of guidance and comfort to women in all walks of life. Women who need a little reminder that they are worthy of love—Love from God, their girlfriends and themselves. It is my prayer that as you read the words of this book, you'll find some of yourself in my story and know that relief is in sight.

Girlfriends, there is a way towards healthy, satisfying relationships. You don't have to suffer in loneliness and exhaustion any longer! I don't claim to have all the answers, but as you'll see, I've fought my way through many hurtful and hard seasons, and I believe what I've learned will be helpful to you—just as I have benefited from many others who have graciously shared their stories with me. Our journey is not meant to be walked alone. I'm so glad you're here with me. Let's go!

Part One: YOU
Where It Begins

*"Caring for myself
is not self-indulgence,
it is self-preservation…"*
—AUDRE LORDE [1]

CHAPTER ONE

What Do I Think About Myself?

"Whether you think you can or think you can't —you're right" [1]— HENRY FORD

WHAT WE THINK about ourselves really matters. If we have a negative view of who we are, it's going to affect all of our relationships. It's true! How we see ourselves can create a lens by which we see everything else, so learning to love yourself just as God made you is crucial.

Have you heard the old saying, *"You can't give what you don't have"*? Well, if you don't have a healthy love of self, then it's going to be hard to love others. Now, I know what some of you are thinking, "The Bible says we are to 'die to ourselves' and not *love* ourselves. That would be feeding our ego!" Yes, I've heard that said before, but just hang with me here. I'll get to that in a minute.

God and My Girlfriends

The wonderful Maya Angelou has a quote that says:

"I do not trust people who don't love themselves, and yet tell me, *I love you*. There is an African proverb that says: '*Be careful when a naked man offers you a shirt*'"[2]

Doesn't that make sense? Most cooks don't serve food without tasting it first themselves, right? They need to know that what they are offering will be tasty and nutritious before they give it to someone else. We also don't recommend books without first reading them ourselves. Why would you tell someone to read a book if you don't know whether it will serve that person well? That goes for just about anything in life. We only give away what we have first experienced for ourselves and know it's value. Learning to love God and others truly needs to start with learning to love ourselves well. Like I said earlier—I know what some of you might be thinking. (Especially my friends who, like me, grew up in a more traditional/fundamental type of religious environment.) This seems to go against much of what we have been taught. "*Deny yourself*", "*You are a worthless sinner*" and "*You don't deserve the love of God, yet he loves you anyway*" are all phrases we heard while growing up. Why, even the beautiful hymn "Amazing Grace" says, "Amazing Grace, how sweet the sound—that saved a *wretch like me.*" Are we really wretched?? (Spoiler alert: No, we are not!)

What Do I Think About Myself?

The Bible says this about us:

1. We are made in the image of God—(GEN 1:27)

2. We are "fearfully and wonderfully made"—(PSALM 139:14)

3. We are SO loved by God, "he sacrificed his only son for us"—(JOHN 3:16).

I'll go into more detail in Part 3 of this book, but for now, let me just say that I don't believe we are to look upon ourselves with shame, guilt. and negative self-worth. Instead, we are to hold our heads up high and remember that we are children of God—princesses of the King! And when we believe with all our heart that God loves us, then we know we ARE lovable. We are created to love and be loved. And when we see ourselves the way God sees us, well, how could we *not* love us? :-)

* * *

Change Your Thinking

If we want to learn how to love and nurture ourselves better, we must first start with the mind. God gave us brains for a reason and he wants us to use them! The mind is a powerful thing. It is what we use to process everything that comes to us. We use our minds to decide what is good or bad, true or untrue, safe or dangerous, helpful or harmful. I believe discernment comes when we use the mind in connection to the Holy Spirit.

Romans 12:2 " . . . be *transformed* by the renewing of your mind."

The Greek word for "renewing" is *anakainøsis,* which literally means **renovation.** I recently lived through a very real renovation in 2019. My husband, Mike and I decided to add a new living room addition onto our existing home WHILE WE WERE STILL LIVING THERE. Clearly we had lost our minds when we thought *that* would be a good idea! Mike and I had been looking for 3 years for a new home to purchase but with no luck. So we finally decided that apparently God wanted us to stay put in our little house in Donelson, TN, which is a suburb of Nashville. We had already lived there for 20 years, purchasing it right after we got married. We thought it would be our "starter home"—HA! But here we are, 22 years later . . . not OUR plans, but God's. And we do love it. It's on a quiet, dead-end street, overlooking a horse farm and the Cumberland River. We love our neighbors and the neighborhood. I remember when we bought the house, I thought it was such a special place and I would never want to leave. We couldn't believe we had found this sweet little neighborhood! It felt like we lived out in the country, but was only 10 minutes from downtown Nashville. It was the perfect place to raise our kids and plant down roots. It was home.

What Do I Think About Myself?

However, as time went by, I started seeing my home in a different light. The "magic" had worn off and I became very discontented living there for a number of reasons. It was an older home and it seemed like almost everyday something needed to be fixed. The large yard, which we had seen as a blessing at first, was becoming harder to maintain as we got older. And, as the kids grew up and started bringing spouses and significant others over, it became almost impossible to gather us all together in our small living room. Three kids had now turned into six adults and a grandchild was coming too! We needed to figure out something soon or we would be having Christmas Day outside on the patio in freezing weather! NO ROOM IN THE INN!! Ha. I was seriously ready to walk away from this old house and find something newer, with more space and nothing to fix! —(Of course, any homeowner knows that having a house with "nothing to fix" is a pipe-dream, so clearly I was living outside of reality at the moment).

So, I marched my little discontented self to open house after open house. I scoured the real estate ads for 3 years with no luck. There were a couple of times I *thought* I had found the "perfect house" and although we made offers on both of them, they fell through. Both times, I was crushed. I cried on the couch and dramatically wailed to Mike something like, *"Why does God hate me???"* to which my very patient, but overly sarcastic husband would say with a smile, "I don't know, honey," and then gingerly pat my head before walking away to let me wrestle it out with the good Lord above. Mike knows when to step away from the drama, I'll give him that.

I'll spare you all the details that God and I worked through, but it became very clear to me that God wanted us to stay put in our Donelson home. No other doors were opening—literally! Luckily, God gave me new lenses in order to see my old house with fresh eyes and I truly fell back in love with our little piece of land by the river. Why would I ever want to leave this beautiful little "holler," as one of our first neighbors, Mr. Jennings, used to call it. Now my heart truly wanted to stay in the little house on the dead-end street, because my eyes had been re-opened to seeing all it's value instead of seeing all it's faults. So, in order to make our home a place that would have room for our expanding family, we decided to add on a new living room addition.

It took 3 months to renovate our house into a place we could continue to call "home," and boy howdy. . .it was quite the experience! I'm not sure how renovating one section of the house ends up affecting the entire house, but trust me, it does. Everything was out of place and there was drywall dust everywhere—pounding and sawing and strangers in our home every day. I remember thinking the construction was *never going to end.* (If you haven't figured it out yet, I can be a tad bit dramatic when under stress. Did I mention I have an overly-patient husband? God is good like that). Anyway, although the renovation wasn't easy, and it was messy, it was totally worth it.

What Do I Think About Myself?

Girlfriends, this is similar to what happens to our minds when we "renovate" them as well. We have to tear down some of the bad thoughts that have been living in our heads and replace them with *good* thoughts. Good thoughts about ourselves, our friends and families, and the world around us. It does us no good to live in that dark place in our own heads. We have to rehaul and reshape our thinking and eliminate the toxic thoughts that want to set up shop in our minds. And just like our home renovation, there will be stress and mess when you tear apart any original structure so that a new and more beautiful version of it can appear—but it will be so worth it. I promise.

* * *

Renovate Your Thoughts

So how do we do this? How do we eliminate the toxic thoughts that are hurting us and replace them with helpful and positive thoughts? First off, we listen to the advice from our brother Paul:

> *"Finally, brothers, and sisters, whatever is true, whatever is noble, whatever is right, whatever is pure, whatever is lovely, whatever is admirable, excellent or praiseworthy —think about such things."* [3]

What we dwell on, we will be engulfed in. It's our choice. We can choose to focus on the broken and damaging thoughts that have played out in our head for years. . .OR we can follow Paul's advice and lean into a more positive way of thinking—about ourselves, God, and others.

Studies have shown that many of our toxic thoughts are rooted in something that was said to us in childhood. Maybe someone told you that you weren't smart, or pretty, or talented. . .or lovable. These can be overwhelming thoughts that can make us feel defeated in life right from the start.

But remember, we have the power to **renew our minds.** We can **renovate our thoughts.** And it will serve us well to do the work here. We will be better for it and our loved ones will too.

One of the ways we can do this is by testing our thoughts. Ask yourself, "*Is this **true**?*" Too often our thoughts are just *not* true. But we have listened to lies for so long, (either told to us by others or by ourselves) that we begin to actually believe they are true when they certainly are not. Here is a good question to ask yourself often: *"What is the story I'm telling myself right now?"* Many times, our storytelling has gone awry. History seems to exaggerate things. Have you ever noticed how a friend might tell a story that you've heard them tell many times . . . and yet, each time the details seem to grow just a little bit. The drama seems to increase with each re-telling of the tale and the villains get

What Do I Think About Myself?

more evil and the victims more pitiful (or more heroic). We all do this at times, but when we change our own stories in our head to fit our agendas, that is when we can really get into trouble.

If you aren't sure if your thoughts are true anymore, ask a trusted confidant if they believe them to be true. Be willing to listen and trust in what they are saying. Sometimes others can see the truth in our lives much clearer than we can. Please take note that I said to ask a "trusted confidant." This must be someone that you deeply trust. Someone you know loves you and has your best interest at heart. If you don't feel like you can trust anyone that well right now, then I encourage you to confide in a professional therapist. I have been served well by wonderful counselors and therapists in the past and I highly encourage you to seek out professional guidance in these matters.

The bottom line is this: we must learn to think *right* and *true* about ourselves and others. Thinking right means we allow accuracy, appropriateness, and truth to set the bar. It means we fight against wallowing in negative self-talk and self-pity. It means we take back control of our own truth about who we are and what we are becoming. We must use our MIND to re-train our thoughts.

I love this quote from Priscilla Shirer: *"Taking thoughts captive means controlling them instead of letting them control you."* [4] Girlfriends, we have the ability to wake up each and every day with a determination to be the boss of our own thoughts and choose positivity over toxicity. We owe it to ourselves and those around us to make that choice.

We must remember: Self-care starts with the mind. Choose to take control of your thoughts today and start becoming the person who God created you to be!

Reflections

1. When you think of yourself, what adjectives do you use? Are they mostly negative? (not good enough, ill-equipped, unlovable, dumb, unattractive, unwanted) If so, what positives can you replace them with?

2. Meditate on the 3 Bible verses listed: Gen 1:27, Psalm 139:14, John 3:16. Which verse speaks the most to you? Memorize it and say it out loud daily.

3. What's one thing you can do today to begin the process of renovating your thoughts toward positivity?

What Do I Think About Myself?

4. Think about what stories you might be telling yourself that are untrue. Replace that with truth.

5. Prayerfully consider who your "trusted confidant" might be to help you with any of the steps above. You don't have to do this alone. There is power in relationship!

CHAPTER TWO

Self-Care

*"Self-care is giving the world the best of you,
instead of what's left of you."* [1]
—KATIE REED, blogger, speaker, mental health advocate

AS A TOURING MUSICIAN most of my adult life, I have spent a lot of time in airplanes. Anyone else who has done much flying would also be quite familiar with the safety instruction demonstration that the flight attendants go through at the beginning of every flight. They quickly show us how to buckle our seat belts, the location of the nearest emergency exits, and also how to use our seat cushion as a flotation device. Then they go over something *very* important: They tell us what we should do if we were to lose cabin pressure and the oxygen masks are suddenly dangling in front of us from the cabin ceiling. Each airline goes about this procedure a bit differently, but there is one thing that each and every airline says *every single time*. The sentence is: **"Should the aircraft lose**

cabin pressure and you need to use the oxygen masks in front of you, always put on your own oxygen mask first before assisting others around you." I've heard this sentence literally hundreds of times, but it really struck me how profound it is on a recent flight. Yes, that's right. Put on your own mask *first*. But wait!!—Shouldn't you help your child put on his/her oxygen mask first before you worry about yourself? Shouldn't you help the elderly person in your row before you selfishly think of yourself? Shouldn't you look around and make sure everyone else is ok before *you* are ok? NO, NO, NO! Why? Because you can't help *anyone else* if you are lying dead on the floor. Sounds harsh, but it's the truth. And unfortunately, that is what happens to many of us. In our attempt to help *everyone*, we end up damaging ourselves to the point that we can't help *anyone.*

* * *

The Big Myth

SO . . . the very first thing I want to address is the big myth about self-care. The myth that self-care is selfish. Repeat after me: SELF-CARE IS **NOT** SELFISH. It's actually one of the least selfish things you can do. Taking care of yourself will only make you stronger and better, not just for yourself, but for everyone else in your life. Family, friends, co-workers. Heck, even strangers will benefit from you becoming the best version of yourself that you can be!

Self-Care

I'm not really sure when this myth started and took hold so strongly. It's pretty rampant in certain religious circles, but we also see it being more pervasive in women, much more than in men. Maybe because females are the "nurturers." I have many girlfriends (I'm looking at YOU Enneagram 2's and 9's!) that seem to easily fall into the trap of taking care of everyone around them first and foremost. And then, if there is any time or energy left to give, she *might* try to do something for herself now and then.

Girlfriends, *hear me loud and clear*: We need to stop putting all our needs on the back-burner of our lives. That is not serving us well! Why? Well, for one thing, it can cause bitterness and resentment towards those around us. Every human being has needs and wants that need to be met. If we leave it up to our family or friends to always meet those needs, and then they don't do it, then what happens? We feel sad, overlooked, unfulfilled, unimportant—*unseen*. It's a bad place to be. And truth be told, many times our loved ones have no idea they aren't meeting our needs because we haven't told them what we need. Also, too often our needs and wants have been buried so long and so deep that **we** don't even know what we need anymore! We just have these longings in our hearts that we have gotten so out of touch with and don't know what to do with because we are afraid that to express them would be, well . . . *selfish*.

Why would it be considered selfish to admit that we are human just like everybody else? And we have needs that need to be met . . . *just like everybody else??* The more we deny our needs, the more we fall into unhealthy spaces, and that just won't end well for anyone. So instead of denying our needs, let's learn how to take care of ourselves so that the burden is lifted off of the shoulders from those around us.

See now? That doesn't sound selfish at all, does it?

* * *

Where do I start?

Before I talk about what self-care looks like, I want to address what self-care *isn't*.

When I ask women, "What does self-care look like to you?" I get a variety of answers. Things like:

"A long massage"

"A much needed pedicure"

"Happy Hour with some friends"

"Spa Day"

"Beach time"

While I do agree that those sound lovely and are great things to do for yourself now and then, self-care shouldn't stop there. Self-care isn't always about pampering yourself. Now don't get me wrong, pampering can be a good thing to do now and then. I would never discount how a nice relaxing pedicure might help bring a bit of temporary peace and happiness in the middle of a hard day. There have been many days that I felt a little lighter walking out of a nail salon after a good foot massage and a new bright color of paint slapped onto my toes. It's almost as if my feet are smiling up at me and saying, "Thank you! We feel better now!" No, I am not dismissing the temporary high of pretty toes. That is REAL.

However, the self-care that I am talking about *here* goes well beyond pampering. It's the kind of self-care that isn't easy, but yields much bigger, long-lasting results than a fun happy hour or a lazy day on the beach. *Real* self-care is doing the things that will make you a stronger, more capable, over-all better human being. Maybe the kind of self-care you need is calling that therapist you've been meaning to make an appointment with for so long, but just haven't found the emotional energy to dive in. Maybe it's driving down to the local recovery meeting and addressing why you can't seem to stop numbing yourself with alcohol or drugs. Maybe it's finally enrolling in those classes down at the local college to pursue that degree you've always wanted. Maybe it's learning your Enneagram number and spending a little time each day working on your strengths and weaknesses in order to know yourself better. Later in this book, I'm going to talk about how we can't really love God if we don't really *know* God, and it works that way with us too. How can we love ourselves if we don't know ourselves?

Speaking of the Enneagram, I'd like to take a moment to talk about how truly helpful it has been for me personally and for many others around me. What is the Enneagram, you say? It's an age-old system of self-discovery. It takes you on a journey of understanding about yourself—what makes you tick, why you do the things you do, and how you can break bad patterns that might be holding you back from following your dreams and becoming everything God created you to be. It's really a remarkable tool. Think of it as free therapy!

The Enneagram breaks down the 9 distinct personality types, one of which will be our basic personality type, but it's common to find a little bit of each type in us all. I've heard some people resist finding their Enneagram number with the excuse that "it puts me in a box." That is actually not true. What it DOES is help you get OUT of the box you have put yourself in! I seriously can't tell you how helpful it is and I want to encourage you to find your number and understand it. Learning about yourself and your true motivations behind your actions might be a little scary and revealing, but it's also amazingly important.

Franciscan Friar, author and speaker, Richard Rohr wrote a book called *The Enneagram: A Christian Perspective* which has been very helpful to many. He has been a huge proponent of the Enneagram and has used it for years in

Self-Care

his ministry and counseling. He often talks about the spiritual fruit of humility and how genuine self-discovery can lead to a healthy dose of humility. Humility doesn't mean that we think less of ourselves. It means we have a healthy appraisal of exactly who we are. . . no more and no less. This is very important for our souls and egos, which of course we all have. Look, getting to know ourselves can be scary. Trust me, I know. The kind of internal work that helps make us better, stronger people isn't easy, but it's so worth it!

Ok, I'm going to stop gushing about the Enneagram right now. You can google it if you want more information (and I hope you do!). But my point is this: There are many tools out there to help you learn how to improve and care for yourself that are absolutely FREE, so the only thing that's stopping you from working on being your best self is . . . well . . . you. Get out of your own way and BEGIN the journey!

The truth is, what real self-care looks like will vary from person to person. It depends so much on your current circumstances, your past experiences and your cultural situation. However, in the next few chapters, we will discuss just a few things that might be helpful for you to get started moving in a good self-care direction.

Reflections

1. Think about why you may feel like your needs shouldn't be prioritized. Are they voices in your head? Or possibly other voices around you?

2. If you are being influenced by other negative voices around you, think about healthy ways to silence those influences.

3. List 3 reasons why you *should* take care of yourself:

4. Changes in our thinking doesn't happen overnight. For real changes to occur, they usually need to be slow and incremental in order to become habits. Think of just 2 small ways you could start implementing more self-care into your daily routine.

5. Is there something besides your own thought patterns that you need to address in order to start caring for yourself properly? Again, consulting with your trusted confidant or therapist might help you see other roadblocks in your life.

CHAPTER THREE

Limits

"In societies no less than individuals, acknowledging our limitations may ultimately be more humane than denying them." [1] —STEVEN PINKER

SEVERAL YEARS AGO, I went on a 4-week non-stop international tour with pop-legend, Christopher Cross. You guys remember, "Sailing", "Ride Like The Wind" or "Arthur's Theme", don't you? I love Christopher and I love his music, so this was a dream job for me. I shouldn't say "was" because as I'm writing this book, it still IS a dream job for me. I'm very blessed to get to travel all over the world with CC and his band and crew. They are a great group to hang with and a talented group to play good music with. Traveling with them is always fun, but at times it can also be exhausting.

On this particular tour, we started in Lima, Peru and

included cities in Chile, Argentina, Brazil, New Zealand and finally 2 weeks in Australia. We did 20 shows in 28 days, which means we were either performing or traveling almost every single day. The "rest" days were few and far between. By the time we arrived back in the United States, we were all exhausted.

I remember the exact moment when the wheels of the plane touched the ground in Nashville, TN and I realized I was home. I immediately started to cry. I couldn't quite figure out *why*— because I loved my job, I loved the people I traveled with, and I loved traveling. My husband came to pick me up at the airport and as I got in the car, the tears were still flowing. He looked at my weepy eyes and said, "*What's wrong, honey?*" I suddenly blurted out, "*I am just **so tired!!**"* I went home that day, put on my pajamas, and I don't think I got out of them for 3 or 4 days straight. I'm not even sure I took a bath! (apologies to my family). I really didn't feel my "normal self" for several weeks. I mean, I was *spent*. And that was when I realized that something had to change, or I was going to be good for nothing and no one.

Yes, human beings have limits. Knowing when we need to REST is critical to our well-being. It's crucial for our physical, mental, emotional and spiritual health. We don't have unlimited power, stamina, or energy, and you know what? *God made us that way for a reason.* Think about that for a minute. Yes, God made us this way for a reason.

The message of rest is found over and over again in the Bible. Look at Isaiah 30:15 for starters and read it out loud to yourself:

> *"This is what the Sovereign LORD,*
> *the Holy One of Israel, says: 'In repentance*
> *and rest is your salvation; in quietness*
> *and trust is your strength,*
> *but you would have none of it."*

Did you hear what you just said to yourself?? "In repentance and REST is your salvation: in quietness and trust is your strength." Resting is how we *renew*. It's how we renew our strength, and more importantly, our relationship with our Creator. We can't commune with God when we are constantly going and doing. Sometimes, God calls us to just BE. He calls us to just *be with him,* doing nothing else but being in quiet stillness so we can hear God's voice and feel his presence. That is the only way we stay connected to our true Source of light, love and energy.

I have often heard it said that "We are human beings, not human doings." That makes so much sense. We weren't made by God to work our fingers to the bone. We were made by God for relationship with him. . .and in order to do that, we must take the time to stop and be still. Psalm 46:10 says it beautifully: "*Be still and know that I am God.*" Hopefully, you do that every single day.

After I had my breakdown from exhaustion, I decided it was time to make a few changes in my life. One of them was implementing "Pajama Day" once a month. It may sound a little silly, but those small intentional times of rest can really make a difference.

Now, you may laugh, but I take my pajama days very seriously! I put them in my calendar, days or even weeks in advance. Just seeing them in my calendar and knowing I have a day scheduled for me to rest is a beautiful thing. It actually helps get me through extra hectic days and weeks because I can see an end in sight. I also plan for them, making sure I get all my errands done and groceries bought the day before. I take every measure to avoid unexpected things that might pop up and force me to actually get dressed and have to leave my house. My husband and son have learned the importance of Mom's "Pajama Days" as well. They know that somebody better be losing a limb if they need me to get dressed and do anything that day! It's become a little joke around our house about how seriously I take Pajama Days, but they have also seen the difference it has made in my physical and emotional well-being. Seriously, I think everyone needs to plan days of REST in their lives . . . no matter what that looks like to each individual. MY rest days include pajamas, but yours may look entirely different.

Yes, "resting" may look very different from individual to individual. Staying home all day in your pj's may just sound plain boring to some of you. Your idea of rest

Limits

might look more like sitting under a beach umbrella, toes in the sand and a good book in your hands. Or maybe it's spending the day hiking in the mountains, away from all technology. Whatever it takes for you to slow down your mind and disconnect from your burdens for a few hours—I just can't stress enough how important it is for your overall well being.

All that being said, I know there are some women out there working 3 jobs just to keep the lights on, and "rest" sounds like a luxury that they can't afford. I've been there myself, so I get it. There was absolutely ZERO chance of a "pajama day" during those years for me. My message to you weary souls is this: *Get creative*. I promise you can make little changes in your daily schedule to work in some rest. Baby step your way into a more balanced life. This is serious business. If you don't, you are going to crash and burn. I promise you that.

Go to bed a bit earlier, sleep in one morning a week, swap out babysitting time with other Mamas. . .whatever you need to do to allow your body and mind some much needed rest, do it. This isn't an option, it's a necessity!

So, make a plan and find your own way to rest and connect with yourself and God. I promise you, you'll be so glad you did.

* * *

God and My Girlfriends

The Power of "No"

In order to carve out times of rest, you may have to learn how to say a tiny, but powerful word. That word is "no." Some of you may have to reach wayyyy back in your memories to recall that word and what it means because, let's face it . . . too many women have forgotten its power. They stopped using it years ago and now it practically feels like a foreign language.

Let me jog your memories ladies. The word "no" is a powerful tool used by people with healthy boundaries that helps prevent burn-out and exhaustion. Sound intriguing? Lean in closer and let me explain how it works! It's truly a magical little word that can change your life, but many women I know feel uncomfortable saying it. Why? Well, there are several reasons. I think part of the problem is that our culture trains women to be the "meet-ers of all the needs" to everyone around them. Saying "no" doesn't feel nurturing, and many women find their value in taking care of everyone around them, so you can see where the conflict lies.

However, I think if we can reframe what saying "no" actually means, we might be able to lean into the positives that will come with that reframing. Then, I believe we will feel encouraged to develop a new and healthier relationship with that tiny, but powerful little word.

In Lysa TerKeurst's book, *The Best Yes*, she makes this powerful statement:

Limits

"We must not confuse the command to love with the disease to please".²

BOOM! I'll admit that I spent much of my early years *deep* in the "disease to please." Making others happy fed my ego's desire to be needed, which translated into me feeling loved. I would break my back trying to run around and meet the needs of everyone around me so that they would be happy. (This was the Enneagram 9 in me trying to create peace). Of course, I learned later that this was a vicious cycle, because a human being's happiness is always short-lived. If we can each do our own hard soul-work, we can learn to sustain JOY. *Happiness*, on the other hand, is a temporary emotion.

I've also learned that someone else's happiness shouldn't be dependent on me. That's something we all have to create for ourselves. But I didn't understand this when I was younger and in my own search for acceptance and love. I spent my energies trying to meet the needs of everyone I met, hoping they would love me. That definitely sounds like a disease! The sad part is that I finally realized that having someone love me because of what I provided them was not real love. They didn't love me for ME. They loved me because of how I made them feel or what I could do for them, but that was NOT real love. Saying yes to everyone around me, no matter what, wasn't healthy for me *or* them, and it led me to remain in toxic relationships for far too long.

God and My Girlfriends

As far as learning *how* to say "no" . . . well, there are many great books out there with helpful advice. *Boundaries* by Henry Cloud and John Townsend was an excellent resource for me. There are healthy and loving ways to say "no" that can benefit everyone involved. Look at it this way: When you say "yes" to something that maybe isn't in your skillset, you are blocking the opportunity for someone else who might be better qualified to get to say "yes." Does that make sense?

Here's an example: Years ago I started attending a new church and I was anxious to serve in any role that the church needed. Being that I have spent much of my time in Nashville as a professional singer, it was a natural fit for me to serve on the music/worship team, so that was where I started. I also had a friend who was working in the "Kid's Place" area who said they really needed some extra help in the preschool classes. Even though I have zero experience with preschool age children (except with my own kids of course, but truly in my case "it took a village"), I said I would sign up to help. Honestly, I thought that there would be other volunteers to REALLY be in charge of all these littles running around and I would just be there for support. This was happening in a very busy season of my life and so it came as no surprise that I accidentally booked myself to sing the special music (a single song right before the sermon) on the same day I was scheduled to work in the preschool class. Rather than have to tell either of them "no," I decided that I could just show up to help in the Kids Place and when it came time during the service for

Limits

the special music, I would just slip out of the preschool class for 5 mins and sing the song. Then I could hop right back over to the preschool class and no one would even know of the conflict! Sounds like a good plan, right?

Wrong. What I didn't anticipate happening was that the other 2 ladies who were supposed to help in the preschool room that day both called in sick at the last minute! So there I was in a panic, with 5 preschoolers staring at me to entertain them and me having no idea what to do. . . AND knowing I'm supposed to be on stage in the auditorium in about 15 mins to sing the solo for the service. So what did I do? The only thing I knew to do. I literally marched 5 little kids onto the stage with me, had them sit on the floor near the piano player. . .I sang my solo. . .and then marched them back down to the classroom! The congregation went from looking incredibly confused at my walking onstage with 5 little ones in tow to howling with laughter as I explained my embarrassing situation. Of course, the kids were cute and funny as they found their parents in the congregation and spent most of my song waving to all their family in the pews. Luckily, it ended up being a funny way to show the members of the church that we REALLY needed more volunteers to help out! That week we had a big influx of volunteers sign up for the nursery and Kids Place. And the Pre-K director sweetly told me *"You're off the hook"*—understanding that I had clearly over-reached with my skills and my schedule.

Funny thing is, a good friend of mine who LOVES

working with young children said, "*Gosh, I wish I had known they needed more help. If they had asked me, I would have really enjoyed serving, but I thought they had it covered!*" Yes, she thought it was covered because I had signed up for it. . .so technically it WAS covered. It was just covered by someone already overworked and out of her skill set. My saying "yes" to that slot, kept her from getting to say "yes" to that slot. . .and it ended up in disaster. All because I didn't have it in me to say "no."

Now, don't get me wrong, there are many times in life we should say a resounding YES! When you have an opportunity to follow your dreams or the ability to use your specific passions and skill sets—those situations almost always call for a "yes"! But learning to accurately evaluate how much time and energy you have to give to each request that comes your way is an important skill. And with that, learning *how* to say "no" is crucial too. You can say something like:

"Thank you for thinking of me! I wish I could say yes, but right now I just don't think I have the time to give to _____ that would serve you well. I'd be happy to _____ instead, if that would be helpful."

Maybe you can offer to reach out to someone else you think might be interested. Or maybe there is something else related to the request that you could help with. Saying "no" doesn't necessarily mean you can't help with the request at all, it just means you can't fill that role the way they have asked.

Limits

For instance:

"I'm so sorry, but no, I can't bake 10 homemade pies for the class bake sale by Friday. . .BUT . . .

Option #1: I could pick up some pre-baked pies from the grocery store and deliver those by Friday. Would that be okay?"

OR

Options #2: I could bake 4 pies. Would that be helpful?

Options #3: I'll be glad to call some of the other mothers for you and see if one of them can help!"

Are you getting the idea here? Offer to do what you *can* —within your own comfort zone, energy level, scheduling ability and skill set. Everyone will benefit from that. . .I promise! It really isn't unloving to say "no." Just remember— when you say "no" it could be a big blessing for the person who now gets to say "Yes"! It's a win/win for everyone.

Human beings have limits. YOU have limits. And that's not a bad thing. Don't think of this as some kind of deficit. That's not it at all. Learning our limits is part of being self-aware, and it helps us develop good boundaries. It can truly be one of the best things you can do for yourself and for everyone else around you.

Reflections

1. When was the last time you felt exhausted? What contributed to that exhaustion?

2. Some messages in our society equate "resting" with "laziness." How does Isaiah 30:15 contradict that message?

3. What does "rest" look like to you? If you struggle with answering this question, think about what rejuvenates you. Anything that fills us back up, rather than depleting us could be considered restful.

4. Do you struggle with saying "no"? Think of one thing you could say no to this week that might lighten your load a bit. When you imagine that scenario, do you feel relieved? :-) If you do, then it's a hard "no"!

5. What are other areas in your life where you need to strengthen your boundaries? Again, maybe your trusted advisor can help speak truth in this area to you.

CHAPTER FOUR

Seasons

"There is a time for everything, and a season for every activity under heaven." —Ecclesiastes 3:1

ONCE WE LEARN that we all have limits, then the next step is learning how to prioritize well. We must be able to decide who and/or what needs our attention the most and make sure we prioritize those needs. If we don't learn to prioritize well, we will almost always end up overcommitted, stressed out, and exhausted.

Something that has helped me learn to prioritize better is understanding that life truly is broken up into seasons. I have gone through seasons of learning, seasons of teaching, seasons of caregiving, and seasons of being cared for. I've had seasons of career highs, and career lows. Seasons of health and high energy, and of sickness and low energy. Busy seasons, slow seasons, happy seasons, sad seasons. And you know what? None of those seasons lasted forever.

God and My Girlfriends

All things eventually come to an end, no matter how good or how bad. As it says in Ecclesiastes 3:

> *There is a time for everything, and a season for every activity under heaven:*
>
> *a time to be born and a time to die,*
>
> *a time to plant and a time to uproot,*
>
> *a time to kill and a time to heal,*
>
> *a time to tear down and a time to build,*
>
> *a time to weep and a time to laugh,*
>
> *a time to mourn and a time to dance,*
>
> *a time to scatter stones and a time to gather them,*
>
> *a time to embrace and a time to refrain,*
>
> *a time to search and a time to give up,*
>
> *a time to keep and a time to throw away,*
>
> *a time to tear and a time to mend,*
>
> *a time to be silent and a time to speak,*
>
> *a time to love and a time to hate,*
>
> *a time for war and a time for peace.*

So, if you find yourself in a good season right now, where you feel you are living your best life, you better enjoy it, because girlfriends, it won't last. Sorry to be the party

Seasons

pooper here, but nothing great will stay great indefinitely. That's just not how life works on this side of eternity. However, the good side of this means that the bad, disappointing, hurtful, painful, mournful times won't last either. Life is a constant ebb and flow, push and pull, up and down, here and there. The seasons are constantly changing and we must learn how to deal with that.

Once I learned this lesson about changing seasons, I found that I could actually appreciate something about each and every season that came my way. Even the hard ones. Remembering that nothing is permanent made it much easier for me to accept where I was and learn from that experience or that season—lessons that would serve me well later on down the road. And what about the fun, happy, easy seasons? Well, those became even more enjoyable as I learned to live in the moment and truly appreciate those times, knowing that they too were only temporary in the grand scheme of things.

Back in 2006 I got a call from my 83 year old Dad, who still lived in Arkansas with my Mom, asking me if I could find some time to come home. I knew something had to be wrong, as he never called to ask me that. As soon as I arrived at their house, I knew there was a problem. The house was a mess and quite frankly, almost disgusting. I had been living in Nashville, TN, for many years at this point, and since my parents were retired, they came to visit us in Nashville several times a year. They always enjoyed the trip, so we rarely went back to their home for visits.

God and My Girlfriends

It had probably been 2 or 3 years since I had been inside their house, and I was floored at their living condition. I will spare you the details here, but trust me when I tell you that no one wants to see anyone living like that. That's when I realized that my mother's dementia had gotten so advanced that she wasn't able to clean and care for the home properly. Not only that, but she was preventing Dad from hiring any outside help because she was under the impression that they couldn't afford it and would run out of money. This wasn't true, but dementia can cause you to believe things that aren't true and become paranoid.

I understood immediately why Dad called me to come home. He knew that once I saw the situation for myself, I would understand the urgency. No one can explain something like that over the phone. My Dad was too proud to ask for help, but he knew he wouldn't have to ask once I saw it first-hand. He knew I would just act. And I did. I immediately started making plans to move them to Nashville, so I could help take care of them both.

I quickly found a wonderful assisted-living facility just about a mile from my house (that was a HUGE blessing!) and moved them into a cute little apartment that became their home for their final years. We were able to be a big part of their daily lives, and I became their main caretaker until Mom passed away in 2013, and then Dad left in 2015.

What I didn't know when Dad made that initial call to me in 2006, was that I was about to enter into a brand-new

Seasons

season of my life. I had been living in a busy season of a career high for several years. I was writing professionally, touring with several country artists, working as a studio singer and really enjoying my work in the music business. It was a high-energy, fun, creative season. But much of that changed once I realized I needed to have space in my life to care for my aging parents. And I'll be honest and admit that it wasn't an easy change for me. However, our plates can only be so full. If you keep piling more food on top of a plate that's already full, something's gonna fall off. I knew that I just couldn't add taking care of my parents on top of everything else I was juggling. So, I pulled way back on my career demands and opportunities and entered into a new season. A season of caregiving. And you know what? Even though I was initially sad that I had to make so many changes to a life I was enjoying, those years turned out to be some of the sweetest and most precious of my whole life. I learned how to slow down and enjoy some simple pleasures again. Even something as simple as walking slowly and looking around at the world as you pass it by. Doesn't that sound so simple that it almost feels silly? But I remember the day that lesson hit me like it was yesterday. I had picked my Daddy up to take him to a doctor's appointment and he was walking very slowly, as he did the last few years of his life. Of course, for someone who was used to a very fast-paced life, I was struggling with not getting agitated and wanting to hurry him up. Then I stopped for a minute and looked up at the sky. It was so gorgeous that day and I found myself thinking:

God and My Girlfriends

"Gosh, the sky is so blue and vibrant! Is this unusual for it to look this blue? Or have I just not noticed it before?"

And that's when I realized that I probably hadn't stopped to look up at the sky in years. Seriously . . . like *years*. Pitiful, huh? So after that realization hit me, I glanced up at the trees and noticed how green the leaves were that day. Then I noticed two birds playfully chasing each other around a bird bath in the garden and how the gardens were so beautiful, and it made me wonder who did their gardening. I was suddenly struck at how much of the world I miss when I always walk so fast—strictly focused on where I am going and never looking at what I'm passing right by. I was jolted out of my new appreciation for the world around me by my sweet Daddy calling back to me, "Hurry up! I'm leaving you!" HA. I had stopped so long in my newfound stupor that he had made it all the way to the car and was waiting on me, for once.

From that day on, I tried to walk slower, even when I was alone. Walk slow and look around. See what God has put on display for me each day. I'm embarrassed to say I spent years missing most of it because I was only focused on getting to my next destination and not appreciating the journey.

So I went from a productive, fast-paced, busy season in my life to a much slower one. A slower one that ended up transitioning into a deeply painful one when I had to say goodbye to them both. First Mom and then Dad, burying them side by side at Woodlawn Cemetery. Other seasons

Seasons

have come and gone since then, but I notice them now. I understand the transitions are needed and necessary, and sometimes they even repeat themselves.

A few years ago, a talented, young singer-songwriter called me one day in tears because she had just discovered that she was pregnant with her first child. While she and her husband were happy about becoming parents, she also confided in me that there was a little part of her that was a bit depressed about it. She had just started having some momentum in her music career and she was afraid this unexpected baby was going to derail all her career hopes and dreams.

"Everything I moved to Nashville to accomplish might be down the drain now," she sadly expressed to me.

"No," I told her, *"That's not how God works. God has a plan for you, and just because this baby wasn't in your plans, doesn't mean it wasn't in God's plans. God created you with your talents and your passions and He's not going to take away your dreams because you are having a family!"*

I mean, really . . . can you see God saying "Oh crap! I had a bunch of plans to bless you in your career, but then you had to go and get pregnant and ruin everything! Darn it! Oh well . . . I guess that's it for you then." Nope. We aren't so powerful that we can ruin God's plans.

"Plus," I told her, *"just because you might have to put your*

career aside for a little while and make this baby a priority, doesn't mean you won't be able to get your career back on track when the time is right."

And you know what? That's exactly what she did. She took a little break, had her baby (and actually had two more babies!) and after a season of being a stay-at-home mom with 3 little kids, she started writing and singing again. Now the kids are all in school and she is thriving as a songwriter in Nashville. She has a career AND a beautiful family! God works things out for our good...always.

But back to seasons and how they help us prioritize. I look at God's meteorological seasons as a guide for myself. Our lives have these seasonal cycles that you will see repeating themselves over and over during our lifetimes. Again, it's just a reminder that if you don't like the season you are in right now, just hang on...no season will last forever, but ALL seasons are needed for our growth into mature human beings. Here is the breakdown as I see them:

Spring: *A time for planting and new growth.* I think back on all the "springtimes" of my life, and I can immediately think of times I was starting something new. Springtimes are exciting but also can be filled with anxiety. Remember going off to college and leaving home for the first time? Getting married and beginning a new life as a couple with your new spouse? Starting a new job? Moving to a new town? All those were exciting and adventurous times, but they also were filled with lots of storms, just as the meteorological spring brings us. Yes, there are many different times in my life I can point to as a "spring season." And then those times fell into . . .

Summer: *A time for nurturing and developing new growth.* We are settled into our new opportunities or experiences and now it's time to watch them flower and grow into whatever we can make them become. Summer is usually a satisfying and motivating time, but it's usually an extremely busy time for us. Summers can be overly hot and dry without enough water and before we know it, we are thirsty and burned-out. Thankfully those over-worked summer seasons lead into . . .

Fall: *A time for harvesting what you have nurtured.* Girlfriends, I don't know about you all, but I LOVE FALL. It's my absolute favorite season. The cooler air comes in and refreshes us, reminding everyone that it's ok to stop and slow down just a bit. The hard work from the summer season is about to be put on display as your "harvest." It's a satisfying time, if you can force yourself off of the proverbial merry-go-round that we usually resist jumping off. Slowing down is hard for many people, but it's necessary throughout our lifetimes. One of the reasons I think people might resist the fall season is because they know what's next. . . .

Winter: *A time of rest and renewal.* When you describe winter as a time of "rest and renewal" it doesn't sound so bad, does it? But for many, winter is just pure hell.

Unfortunately, many of our winters are forced upon us via a traumatic event. A job loss. A divorce. An illness. A death of a loved one. Life will force us into slower modes sometimes and it isn't fun. But if we try to realize that it can come with benefits for our overall health, sometimes it's easier to take.

I'm actually writing this chapter as I sit at home recovering from Covid-19. Just in case you have been living on Mars for the last few years and don't know, Covid-19 is a horrible virus that spread throughout the world in 2020. My husband and I both did everything we could to stay safe during that time of pandemic, but unfortunately we both ended up contracting the virus and it hit us both hard. The pandemic itself was difficult, causing havoc across the globe. So many people's lives were turned upside down, including ours. Not being able to go out in society and be our productive selves was hard enough, but add actually *getting* Covid-19 into the mix and well. . .my husband and I are both feeling pretty beat up right now.

"What are you doing?" my husband just asked me as he hobbled into the living room, taking a break to move his body after days of lying in our bed, feeling miserable.

"I'm working on my book. I'm writing a chapter on seasons today." I replied.

"What season would you call this?" he said as he looked at me with that pitiful look that someone who is just *over it* gives you.

Seasons

"I'd say it's a winter. A long, harsh winter," I replied.

"That sounds about right," he said sadly.

"But hey," I inserted, putting on my best Pollyanna face, "We won't appreciate the springtimes without the winters!"

He stared at me for a long time and then with all the positivity he could muster at that moment he said, "*If you say so*," and went back to bed. Poor fellow.

How many of you can relate to his excitement about winter? Whether you want to believe it or not, winters are necessary, and they ARE a part of life. Fighting against them will only make it harder for you. We must learn to embrace the hard times as well as the easy ones and remember that good can come out of those difficult seasons. Sometimes just as much, if not even more so, than the easy ones.

The bottom line is that God works in ALL seasons. Accepting whatever season is happening around you at the time is crucial. My pastor calls it "consenting" to what is happening around you. If we fight against it all the time, we are just making it so much worse on ourselves. We can either consent to whatever is happening, good or bad, and walk through it with complete trust that God is walking along with us—or we will white knuckle ourselves right into a complete meltdown. Some might use the term "surrendering". It's actually very *freeing* when we can get to that place. God will walk us through all our seasons, so no matter what season you find yourself in, just relax and remember two things.

It won't last forever.

God is in it with you. You are not alone.

Recognizing your season will help you prioritize. Not everything can be of equal importance to you all the time, and it's ok to set some things aside while you take care of the things God is calling you to do, for *this* season.

Reflections

1. Do you feel like you have trouble prioritizing things in your life? Meditate on what might be contributing to that issue. Is it time management? Disorganization? Too many commitments? Or something else?

2. What season do you feel like you are in right now?

3. What is one thing that might help you enjoy your current season better?

Seasons

4. Think back on a fun, joyful season in your life. How long did it last? Did you take the time to appreciate it while you were in it?

5. We discussed two truths to help us through hard seasons:

   a) No season lasts forever

   b) God's in it with you. You are not alone.

Which truth gives you the most comfort right now? And why?

CHAPTER FIVE

Your Story Matters

"Owning our story and loving ourselves through that process is the bravest thing we'll ever do." [1]
—BRENE BROWN

IT IS SO EASY to look at other people's lives, other people's stories, and compare ours to theirs, but comparing our stories *just isn't helpful*. No two stories could possibly be the same. We have all walked unique paths since the day we were born. You are creating your very own story with each choice you make and with each opportunity that you take or don't take. Spending your time in comparison to others is a dead-end road. We will talk more about this in Chapter 7, and how it can ruin a good friendship if we aren't careful. But for now, let's just talk about how spending time comparing ourselves to others affects us, (trust me, it's NOT good self-care!)—and what we can do to avoid falling into that pit-trap.

God and My Girlfriends

First off, I believe that one of the most effective ways to stop the comparison game is to own our own stories—own them and believe that our stories *matter*. When we stay focused on using our own stories to help others, we don't have time to compare ourselves, our stories, or our work to those around us.

The truth is, no two lives are the same. God made every single one of us unique. Speak these statements out loud:

I am uniquely ME and no one else can be *(insert your name here)*.

I need to remember how much care and intention God took in creating *(insert your name here)*.

Only I can live the life God intended for *(insert your name here)* to live!

Doesn't that make you feel kind of special?? You aren't some random creature that spontaneously happened with no reason and no purpose! Nope. You are YOU for a reason.

Psalm 139:

Oh yes, you shaped me first inside, then out;

you formed me in my mother's womb.

I thank you, High God—you're breathtaking!

Body and soul, I am marvelously made!

Your Story Matters

I worship in adoration—what a creation!

You know me inside and out,

you know every bone in my body;

You know exactly how I was made, bit by bit,

how I was sculpted from nothing into something.

Like an open book, you watched me grow from conception to birth;

all the stages of my life were spread out before you,

The days of my life all prepared

before I'd even lived one day.[2]

Each one of us was designed by God for a very specific reason. When we try to emulate someone else—maybe someone who we think is cooler than we are, or has a better life than we do, or does more important work than we are doing—then we are missing out on the specialness of what God created US to do.

* * *

You have permission to DREAM

Part of owning your story is finding your purpose. Unfortunately, I meet so many women who are struggling with that. One reason behind this struggle is the belief that they don't have the right to have their own dreams and desires. *Not true.* Each human being has the right to follow the dreams that God puts in their heart. I like to call those dreams *passions*.

The passion I am talking about is not the passion you might feel for another human being. I may feel passionate about my husband, but making him my sole purpose in life wouldn't be healthy. He might be a big part of my world, but no other human being should be your whole world. Unfortunately, there are many women who have come from certain religious cultures that are told the exact opposite. They are told by their religious leaders that a woman's entire reason for being here on this earth is to be a helpmate for man. Those women aren't encouraged to have any dreams of their own. Instead, they are programmed to believe that they are simply here to help her spouse follow *his* dreams. We are just the support team. This type of religious teaching isn't just *un*helpful, it's harmful. What about a woman who never marries? Does that mean she has no purpose in this world? It's ridiculous and misogynistic to teach this. If you are in a religion that says that you don't have the right to have your own dreams, or you have no worth if you aren't tied to a man, I'm begging you to re-think your association with that religion. That is a form of enslavement. Jesus came to set us *all* free.

But I digress. Back to finding our purpose in our passions. We can be passionate about an interest, an idea, an activity or a cause. Passions are the things that make us feel alive and give us a real desire for life! They are the reasons we want to jump out of bed each morning and use our talents or gifts to make a difference in this world. Passions are things that bring you intense joy and fulfillment. Things you will fight for!

I've heard many women say that they don't feel like they have any talents/gifts, but I'm here to tell you that if you feel this way, you are WRONG! We are ALL born with talents to use in this world and make it a better place. There is absolutely no human being born without a use, a talent, a gift. Now, I'll admit that some talents may be more obvious than others. I've had many people say they wish they could sing or write songs like me. Yes, I was lucky enough to have my musical talents revealed at a young age, and my parents helped nurture those talents so that as I grew older, I could use them to bring music into the world around me. But trust me, many of you have gifts that I wish I had!!

Years ago, I read a book by Max Lucado called, *Cure for the Common Life.* It was one of those "AH-HA!" books for me. He talks at length about how to find your "sweet spot,"[3] which is the place where your satisfaction intersects with success. The place where your talents and opportunities merge perfectly.

Think back on your life a bit right now. What have you done well in the past? What are the skills you have that your friends regularly call you about for advice or help with? Are you constantly being asked about recipes? Maybe it's because you are gifted in the kitchen! Do you notice that friends are always asking gardening advice? Maybe it's because of those gorgeous flowers in your front yard that bring beauty into your neighbor's world. Do you get called on often for relationship advice? It could be that you are a good listener and have developed a wisdom that others find incredibly valuable. Are you always being nominated to chair a committee, organize a group of volunteers, or take the lead in a project? Sounds like you have the gift of leadership! Finding your gift (or gifts), really does come from being able to honestly analyze your strengths and weaknesses—and that usually comes from how you help others. Just think about the times where you genuinely felt you were being of service to someone. You'll almost always find your gifts connected to where your heart calls you to serve.

A few years ago, I was in my very cluttered and unorganized office and I couldn't find a lyric I needed to sing that day in the studio. I knew I had printed it out somewhere but amidst the chaos on my desk, there was no finding it. I was late to the studio already, desperate to get out the door and I REALLY NEEDED to find that lyric. That was when I admitted to myself that I needed to get some help in that area in my life. I called my friend Amanda, who is a whiz at organizing and decorating. She came over to my house and in just a few hours had completely reorganized my office. Not only was I amazed at how she knew exactly how to tackle my problem and get me some instant relief, but I was also amazed at how much JOY she seemed to get from it! I mean, *who* finds *JOY* in organizing a messy room?? Well, Amanda does! Girlfriends, that is a gift she has that I do NOT. Soon after that, she told me that she was thinking of starting a business on the side, helping people organize their homes. When Amanda had an organizing challenge in front of her, she loved it. So she had the idea of taking her passion and turning it into a business and man, THAT is finding your "sweet spot."

Another friend of mine Sarah, is an amazing cook. She recently retired and was wondering how best to use the newfound extra time on her hands. So what did she do? She started using her gifts in the kitchen to bless those around her. She did this by what I started calling her "cookie ministry". About once a week she delivered cookies to her family and friends, always with a beautiful bible verse on the top of the container as an extra blessing. Not only do I look forward to cookie drop-off days because of the cookies, but also, it's extra special when she has a bit of time to stay and visit. Friendship and cookies! You can't beat that! She also uses her talents to cook meals for those that are sick or homebound. We have been the recipients of her delicious meals several times and let me tell you, her cooking IS a ministry!

Now look, I can organize and I can cook when I need to, but I know enough about myself to say with complete clarity that I am not in my "sweet spot" when I'm organizing and/or cooking! There is a big difference in knowing you are capable of something vs what you are passionate about doing.

God and My Girlfriends

Now I'm about to say something that some of you may not like. It goes against what I hear many motivational speakers say in the self-help world. . .but it's truth, so lean in for a minute and listen up: **You cannot be anything you want to be.**

I know, I know. Some of you are clutching your pearls right now. It goes against what the current self-help mantras are. To clarify—I honestly *do* appreciate the sentiment behind the statement, and the hope it might give to someone out there who feels their situation or circumstances might inhibit them from following their dreams. Many people have fought against the odds to do something that others said they could never do. But part of finding what you are uniquely made to do is being able to honestly assess your gifts and talents.

I was fascinated by ice skaters when I was a little girl, and for a moment, dreamed of being an Olympic Ice Skater. Of course, the fact that I was born as probably the least athletic person *ever* didn't really play out in my dreams at the time. For about a year, I would go to the local ice skating rink and work on my ice skating skills, hoping that some great coach would notice my inherent gift on the ice and call my parents to BEG them to let him coach me straight to the Olympics! After about a year of working on the ice and still never being able to even skate backwards (HA!), I finally realized that this dream probably wasn't in the plans for my life. Another friend of mine wanted to play basketball. . .yet he never grew past 5'7" and so it

Your Story Matters

became clear that being a professional basketball player was probably *not* in the cards for him. I've had several young singers approach me through the years about wanting to become a background singer in Nashville. However, when I met up with them and realized that they had no ear for finding harmony notes, I had to break the news to them that singing background as a profession for them wasn't going to happen.

But HEY! Finding out that you aren't good at something isn't all bad news!! It's actually GOOD NEWS, because it helps you realize that you might need to change your original planned path and go towards something else that you were meant to do. Something you were *made* to do! Eliminating things is part of the process. I've seen family and friends all make adjustments along their life paths, just as I have. It's perfectly normal, so don't get down if something you try doesn't pan out.

Also, there's more good news. Although *"you can not be anything you want to be, you **can** be everything God created you to be"*[4] That's right, you are gifted with exactly the right skill set, gifts and talents to become all that God intends you to be. He's got a plan, and you've got the skills, girlfriend! Isn't that reassuring? God knows what you need to become who you were meant to be. He thought all that through before you were born. Ya'll . . . we are in good hands.

One more thing to remember is that it's not necessarily the

destination that matters, but it's the journey. As we go along our life path, we are creating not just one story, but many different stories along the way. We learn something with each thing we try, whether we succeed or fail. It's about growing and learning and becoming. I've heard it said by many people that God isn't so concerned about what we are *doing* in our lives, as He is about *who we are becoming*. God can use our failures as well as our successes to help mold us into who He has created us to be. And realizing who He created us to be is how we can begin to write our stories.

Yes, we each write our own stories. We write them with each choice we make day to day. We write them in the care we take with our relationships. But mainly we write them by the way we love. The way we love God, our friends, and ourselves.

I recently saw the musical *Hamilton* and was completely blown away. The production, the acting, singing, choreography and dancing—it was all so stellar! But it was the STORY that drove it all. Actually, I should say the *stories*. Although the main character was Alexander Hamilton, it was pointed out to me that Eliza Hamilton's story was told just as profoundly in the musical, and they were right. At the end there is a song that just slays me called "Who lives, who dies, who tells your story." Eliza points out the stories of many of the characters in the play, including her own, and it's a beautiful and moving tribute to the way one life can affect many others.

Your Story Matters

Here is the bottom line: When you remember that your story *matters,* then you'll find it easier to prioritize taking care of yourself, to follow your dreams passionately, and work on becoming the best version of yourself that you can be.

And in doing so, you honor the creation that God so carefully and beautifully made. . .YOU.

Reflections

1. List one thing that is unique about YOU:

2. Do you feel like you have a purpose? Do you think other people have a purpose? Read Psalm 139 out loud and then meditate on that verse. How does it make you feel?

3. What dream have you had, but never felt the confidence to pursue? What is stopping you from living it out?

4. What is something that other people have told you that you do well?

5. Remember that YOU can write your own story. You write it each day with the choices you make. We may not be able to change the past, but we are still in charge of our future! How do you want your story to unfold?

Part Two: GIRLFRIENDS
We Were Made For Community

"A sweet friendship refreshes the soul."
—Proverbs 27-9

CHAPTER SIX

What Do I Think of My Friends?

Whether we sink or swim in life may very well depend on the people we are connected to." [1] — DERON SPOO [1]

NOW THAT WE'VE DISCUSSED how important it is to take care of ourselves, let's talk about how we can better nurture our friendships and why it's so very important that we take the time to do that. Just like a marriage, in order to thrive and continue in a healthy, close relationship, we must nurture friendships. And in case there is any doubt about it, we *all* need friends. We just do. Why? Well, because our Creator, God, made us that way. He made us to seek out relationships—mainly to seek out relationship with Him—but also with each other.

When God created Adam, it didn't take long before God said, "It's not good for Adam to be alone. I'll make him a

God and My Girlfriends

partner."[2] God made Adam in a way that would make him desire community, love and friendship. Still today, human beings crave connection with other souls.

Sadly, medical studies show that loneliness is one of the top public health issues of our time. Some mental health professionals have called it an epidemic,[3] and our recent Surgeon General, Dr. Vivek Murthy, has said it's our #1 current public health crisis![4] Here we are, living in an age where connection is easier than ever; the internet has made the world a much smaller place, yet studies show that loneliness is at an all time high. There has been an especially sharp increase in *women* who suffer from loneliness in the last 10 years . . .

Why is this?

There are several contributing factors to this epidemic.

1. ***Over-scheduling.*** As we grow older, with more responsibilities surrounding our families and jobs (aka "adulting"), we feel we have less and less time for friendships. We have our careers, marriages, kids, and by the end of the day, scheduling time with girlfriends can seem like just another thing on our "to-do" list. We end up putting it off over and over again for another "day when I'm not so busy"— but then that day never happens because we continue with our over-scheduling. It becomes a vicious cycle, one that is detrimental to our relationships.

What Do I Think of My Friends?

2. **Competition.** Sadly, society pits women against each other. I see it in branding and messaging everywhere. We are encouraged by our culture to look at one another to determine how we are doing in our lives. How do we measure up? *"Am I as pretty as she is? Do I dress as cute as she does? Is my house decorated as nicely as hers? Do I throw better parties than she does? Are my kids as popular as hers?"* etc . . . I could go on and on, but you get what I'm saying, right? We look at the other women around us to gauge what we are doing well and what we can improve upon. How are we supposed to connect with someone if we feel we are in competition with them?

3. **Mistrust.** I've had many women tell me that they just don't trust women. It's hard to believe someone would write off an entire gender as "untrustworthy," but I know what they mean. What they are really saying is that they have been hurt by women so many times that now they are afraid to be open and invest in close friendships. I think we've all been hurt by friends in the past. Deeply hurt. I understand why it seems easier to put up a wall around your heart than to do the work that healthy friendships sometimes require.

This leads us back to the initial question: "What do I think of my friends?" You might think that is silly, but hear me out for a minute. Close your eyes and picture each friend that you have in your closest circles. Then ask yourself, "What do I think of her?" It might surprise you. It might also make you reevaluate who you surround yourself with—OR, it might give you a new and stronger appreciation for those you call "friends."

Who we choose to offer our friendship to shouldn't be without thought. I'm not saying you should be stingy with your companionship. Quite the opposite! We should be open to being friends with anyone, but that doesn't mean that you don't instill certain expectations in that relationship. Even boundaries. Otherwise, you might end up feeling #3 above—and hurt because you trusted in someone who wasn't trustworthy.

Here are just a few questions to ask yourself when evaluating your friends:

Is she ***trustworthy?*** Have you shared confidences with her that she has held tightly, showing protection for you?

Does she feel like a ***safe place*** for you? Can you share your honest feelings with her without judgment or ridicule?

Does she live her life with ***integrity***? Is she someone who consistently takes the high road, showing strong moral principles and good judgment of character?

Is she ***loving*** and ***compassionate***? Has she shown empathy and compassion for others, always doing what she can to make life better for those around her?

Do you ***respect*** her? Do you value her advice, because she

What Do I Think of My Friends?

has shown herself to have the qualities of 1–4 above?

My sweet Mama used to always say, "If you hang out with a bunch of turkeys, you'll eventually turn into one yourself. . . or at least people will THINK you are one." Hmmmm . . . perception can be truth to some, right? Anyway, she would always follow it up with, "But if you fly with the eagles . . . well, then you will probably end up soaring too." Although I don't necessarily agree that her assessment of friendship should just be based on that theory, I do agree that who we connect ourselves to can make a major difference in our lives. So, that's why evaluating who you are closest to these days is very important.

* * *

What is a friendship?

Shasta Nelson is the founder of GirlfriendCircles.com, which is a website dedicated to helping women connect and enhance friendships. She came up with an interesting definition of friendship, which I love:

*"A friendship is a mutual relationship between two people that is **satisfying**, **safe**, and where both people feel **seen**."*

We might have many relationships in life that don't qualify as a "friendship" when you go by that definition. For instance, you may have a wonderful relationship with your pastor, or your therapist, or a teacher. You may feel very safe, satisfied and seen by them, but does it go both ways? Often those people know much more about you, than you do about them, right? Those are good relationships to have, but they aren't friendships. It's not reciprocal. Both people in a friendship should feel they can be vulnerable with one another, and I don't know about you guys, but my therapist, as great as she is, doesn't share her intimate feelings with me. I may feel like I know her, because she knows ME. Oh Lordy, she knows me, for SURE! But I don't pay her to tell me what's bothering her. So, while we may have a genuine care and like for one another, it isn't a "friendship." Seeking out reciprocal relationships is what I'm focusing on here.

Speaking of reciprocal, this might be the time to address another important question while we are talking about what makes for a good friendship.

* * *

What kind of friend are you?

Everything that you are expecting from your friends should be something you require from *yourself*. Learning how to *be* a good friend is very important in this equation. You might go back and look at that list of five questions above and see if your friends would find those same qualities in you. Friendship *is* very reciprocal. If you want to

What Do I Think of My Friends?

attract trustworthy and reliable friends, you must offer the same qualities. Good people attract good people. If you make yourself into the kind of friend you want to have, I can promise you that your friendship circles will become exactly what you need them to be.

So, what do you think of your friends? Still struggling with that? Let me tell you what I think of mine and maybe that will help. The friends I have, especially in my closest circle, are honest and loving people of integrity. They have deep wells of compassion and empathy in their hearts. They have shown me they are trustworthy by sharing and holding confidences. They hold me accountable in the most gracious of ways, and they will punch someone in the face who is mean to me. (Ok, I may have over-reached on that last thing, but they DO have my back!) Are they perfect? Nope. Have they hurt my feelings at times? Yep. Have I had screaming matches with a few? Mayyyy-beee??? Yet, we stand strong and stay together because that's what true friends do.

Look, I'm not saying friendship won't be messy some days. No two people are going to agree on everything, but hear me when I say that IT'S OK to disagree with your friends sometimes. You really don't want to build a huge echo chamber in your life with only friends who never disagree with you. Disagreements can lead to deep conversations where you learn from one another and grow. As we work on being better individuals, our friends can help us with that. They can challenge us on certain ways of thinking that might not be true, either about ourselves or the world around us. That's why having a diverse group of friends is so helpful. In the next few chapters, we will dive deeper into how we should approach both making friends and *keeping* friends. We all know that those can be two very different things.

The bottom line is that when you think of your friends, don't expect perfection, or you will be let down. Don't expect them to agree 100% of the time with you either, because unless they aren't being honest with you, that won't happen. And don't expect them to never let you down, because we are all human, and humans mess up. A lot. Just choose quality individuals who bring love, positivity, laughter, honesty and balance into your world, and then cover it all with a huge helping of grace.

Reflections

1. Over-scheduling, feeling competitive, and mistrust are three reasons why some women struggle with feeling lonely. Which of these reasons resonates the most with you? Or, is there another reason that you feel contributes to you feeling more isolated than you'd like to be?

What Do I Think of My Friends?

2. What is one thing you can do to counter-act the reason you listed above?

3. How many people are in your closest circle of friends? Do you feel like each one has the qualities you should expect in a friend?

4. Do you give the kind of friendship you expect in return? What is one thing you can do to become a better friend?

5. How do you feel when you and a close friend can't agree on something? What's a healthy way to work through disagreements?

CHAPTER SEVEN

Friendship Killers

"In the end we will remember not the words of our enemies, but the silence of our friends."
— MARTIN LUTHER KING, JR.[1]

MAKING FRIENDS IS EASY. Developing long-lasting, deep, bonded friendships is harder work. Maybe that's part of the reason too many people tend to settle for the superficial, never-going-below-the-surface relationships. Unfortunately, those connections, while *real,* aren't going to give you the kind of community you are searching for. We all have a deep need to belong. We want to have a close circle of friends that we can do life with that feels safe and secure. Exactly 100% of human beings want that. This is *truth*. Now, some of us may be more independent or introverted than others and don't feel the need to gather in groups as often as the extroverts, but that doesn't mean they aren't in need of a trusting community.

We all want a table to gather around where we can laugh and cry and love one another. A table to celebrate each other's successes or comfort those who are hurting. A table that is full of food and drink that will not only fill our bellies, but our souls. A table where we feel we belong. That's what we all crave—and we can have it! However, in order to nurture that kind of trusting community, we need to be aware of the things that will kill it, or at least deeply maim it.

* * *

The Scarcity Mindset

Comparison is a big friendship killer. It really does us zero good to ourselves or our relationships. When we compare ourselves to the women around us, we either think we aren't as good as they are, which is hard on our self-esteem, OR we decide that we are better than they are. This is equally as damaging to our ego, giving us a false sense of "better than."

I like to think of my circle of girlfriends as buoys in a harbor, all linked together. No one sinks down underneath the water just because another happens to rise. No, it doesn't work that way. We are all tied together, so when the tide rises for one, we all rise! When I live in fear that when someone else rises around me, it will cause me to drown, well . . . that's buying into the "scarcity mindset" and it's so very detrimental to friendships.

Friendship Killers

The scarcity mindset makes us believe that there isn't enough to go around, so if one person is successful, then it limits our ability to be successful too. Y'all, that just isn't true! Just because another sister's light shines does not mean *my* light will diminish. Just because my friend has a moment of success doesn't mean that I won't have success too. And just because a sister is ahead of me in her race, doesn't mean I won't cross my own finish line when the time is right.

We can't truly celebrate each other's joys and achievements if we are nursing the scarcity mindset and bogging ourselves down with comparison. We must stay focused on our own lane and run our own course, while still cheering on the others around us that are running much different races.

Truly. It's ok to clap like crazy for the ladies ahead of you. And I'll bet you'll find them waiting for you at your own finish line, cheering you on as well!

* * *

Envy / Jealousy

I was listening to the "4 Things With Amy Brown" podcast recently and she was interviewing *New York Times* Best Selling Author and Social Activist Glennon Doyle. Doyle was talking about learning to *feel* your feelings and how helpful that practice can be in better understanding yourself. She specifically talked about the green-eyed monster, envy. We are often told how we shouldn't have envy for someone, and that's true, but I loved how Doyle reframed how we should deal with that emotion. When we feel ANY feeling, we should acknowledge it, sit with it, and then maybe even ask it what it is trying to tell us. God made all the emotions for a reason, so maybe, just mayyybeeee, envy is a needed emotion that helps realign us when it pops up.

Doyle made the observation that (usually) when we find ourselves envious of someone else, it's because they are doing something that, deep down in our souls, we know *we* should be doing, but for some reason, we aren't. If we are open to what any of our feelings are trying to teach us/tell us, we can find good in them all. However, when we let envy take root in our hearts, it can be a relationship killer all around.

An honest friend of mine once admitted that she finds it very easy to rush to a friend's side when they are knocked down and hurting—always finding it in her heart to offer compassion, empathy and a shoulder to cry on. But, rushing to celebrate with a friend who had just gotten GOOD news? Well, she found that much harder. I would guess most of us struggle with that from time to time, even on the best of days. If we are caught off guard on an insecure day and a friend calls to tell us her wonderful news, envy can work its way into the equation very easily. We have to remember that envy is usually telling us more about US than it is about our friend, so it's something

Friendship Killers

we need to sit with and address in ourselves before we let it fester and ruin an important relationship in our lives. Getting a hold of envy before it festers is crucial for true friendship.

* * *

I used to think that envy and jealousy were basically the same emotion, but I recently learned that jealousy is actually a very different emotion. In Brené Brown's book, Atlas of the Heart, she explains the distinct difference like this:

"ENVY occurs when we want something that another person has.

JEALOUSY is when we fear losing a relationship or a valued part of a relationship that we already have."

As you can see by those definitions, jealousy can be a friendship killer as well but for a completely different reason than envy. If we are always worried that we will lose a valued friendship to another women, it can cause unhealthy jealousy to fester. No one wants to feel like they are being smothered, covered and owned by someone, whether it's a man or another woman. We have to feel freedom in our relationships in order for them to thrive.

A good check list to go down now and then might look something like this:

1. Does it bother me if I hear a friend praising the attributes of another friend/woman?

2. Do I feel left out if a friend goes to lunch with another friend without me?

3. Do I feel like something might be wrong if I don't hear from my friend at regular intervals?

4. Do I make it a point to let everyone know that a friend is MY "BFF"?

If you answered yes to any of those questions, you might be feeling a bit possessive of your friendship and jealousy could be driving that possessiveness. It's definitely another friendship killer that you need to address. . . pronto!

* * *

Possessiveness

Our friends are gifts to us from God. Just like with anything else in this world, we must hold our gifts with open hands and not closed fists. However, some women find it hard not to be possessive with their close friendships.

Why do we feel possessive of our friends? Well, there are many different reasons this emotion comes up. For one, it usually takes a lot of time and energy to nurture that kind of bond with another human being. If you feel

Friendship Killers

that connection being threatened in some way, either by another person, another interest, or a new job—anything that causes your friend to lose focus on you for a moment, it can be hurtful.

That is why it's important for you to have more than one close friend. One friend cannot be everything you need at all times. It's just not possible. When you set that kind of expectation on them, your friend will likely start feeling burdened. This can lead to your friend needing a break from the relationship, so they might pull away for a bit. That doesn't mean they don't love you or don't want to be your friend, but if you do feel a close friend becoming less available to you, it might be worth taking the time to evaluate what you have been expecting from her and if maybe, just maybe. . .it was too much.

There was a meme going around on social media recently that said something like, "A true friend will always be there for you, no matter what!" That really bothered me because it felt like an unrealistic bar to set for a friendship. I mean, if that is the gauge with which to decide if I'm a good friend or not, I have failed at literally ALL of my friendships! There have been many times that I wished I could have dropped everything and rushed to be with a friend who was sick or hurting, needing help with a project, or even celebrating something. You know, all those "life moments" that you want friends to walk with you through—but my own set of circumstances prevented me from being there.

God and My Girlfriends

For instance, a girlfriend of mine bought her first house recently and was very excited about moving from her little apartment into a place that she could finally call her own. She was closing on a Friday morning and had rented a U-haul for the next day. She needed friends to help her with the logistics of moving all her belongings on that Saturday.

"Can you come help me move that day?"

I looked at my calendar and it was already filled with other commitments.

"I'm so sorry, but I don't have any time that day to help," I said sadly.

Was I not a "true friend" because I couldn't drop everything else in my life and help her on this important day?

I guess she could have said, *"Well, thanks a lot! Way to show up for me when I need you. What could you possibly be doing on Saturday that's more important than helping a friend? Some friend YOU are!"* and hung up the phone.

Thankfully, she didn't feel that way.

"It's ok. I've got several others to call, so I'm sure I'll have enough help."

Then I asked, *"Hey, since I'm not available on Saturday, can*

Friendship Killers

I come over on Sunday and help you unpack boxes, hang up some pictures and start decorating the place a bit?"

"That would be wonderful!" my friend exclaimed.

"Awesome," I said. *"I'll be there at noon with a hammer and a pizza!"*

There have been many other times that I haven't been able to be beside a dear friend on an important day, and vice versa. However, realizing that our friends have other important people in their lives besides us, is really crucial in maintaining a healthy friendship. There is a big difference between making friendships as big priorities in our lives and expecting a friend to make you their TOP priority always. That is a possessiveness that will eventually ruin a friendship every single time.

* * *

The Silent Treatment

I can't tell you how many friendships I've seen damaged simply by bad communication skills. Learning how to express ourselves well is another important part of developing healthy friendships. Unfortunately, when we don't have the tools to express ourselves well, it can often result in another "friendship killer"—which is when we simply don't communicate at all. In other words, we give them The Silent Treatment.

I've done it. I'm not proud of it, but it's true. The reasons behind my silence vary. Sometimes, I go silent because I'm mad about something my friend did, and I don't know how to express myself in a way that will lead to a productive conversation about it yet. Throw in the fact that I've always been someone who avoids conflict at all cost, so what you end up with is. . .silence.

Or I go silent because my feelings have been hurt and subconsciously, I think if I go silent it will hurt them back. Not my proudest admission, but I'm being honest here. Of course, many times, the person I was trying to hurt with my sudden silence didn't even realize I was being silent, which *really* hurt my feelings and made everything much, much worse. Clearly NOT the ideal way to handle hurt feelings in a friendship. Learn from my mistakes here, friends.

Learning to communicate our feelings to our friends is something that we all need to learn how to do better. I know that saying things like, *"You've hurt my feelings," "I feel overlooked,"* or even *"You made me mad"* are not things that are easy to say to anyone, especially a close friend. However, if we are going to avoid giving someone The Silent Treatment, we have to be brave enough to say our truth to our friends. If they really are your friends, they will listen and be willing to have a conversation about whatever is bothering you. Hopefully, a conversation that will end with understanding and forgiveness.

Friendship Killers

The truth is, I have found that my closest bonds with friends have come in those difficult moments. It's when we have honest conflict and work through it together that we come out closer and more bonded than ever. There is a vulnerability that comes when you share your heart with someone. When they show that they still love you and won't abandon you, even after seeing an unflattering side of you, well. . .that's a beautiful thing.

One last damaging side effect of The Silent Treatment is that it leaves room for assumptions. If I go silent on a friend, it leaves her wondering what is going on. Without me telling her what is happening, her only choice is to start imagining different possibilities, which may or may not even be real.

"Maybe she's mad because I haven't returned that dress that I borrowed? Yeah, that MUST be it!"

Then because she feels that's so ridiculous, she thinks, *"Now why wouldn't she just TELL me she wants the dress back? I would have taken it over immediately. That's so silly."*

And now my friend feels she has the right to be frustrated/mad at ME.

I probably had completely forgotten she even HAD that dress! That wasn't it AT ALL. She was wayyyyy off. But because I wasn't communicating the real problem to her, I left the door wide open for assumptions. As a result, her only option was to *guess* what my issues were with her because I wasn't willing to tell her the truth. What a mess, right?

I'm not suggesting that the minute you are hurt/mad/confused/disappointed that you should immediately go find your friend and talk it out. There is definitely an argument to be made that it is healthy to think through your feelings and thoughts before confronting the person who has wronged you. We should be able to say:

"When you did _____, it hurt my feelings. Now I need a little time to myself to work through it."

That is a healthier alternative than just leaving them to wonder why you suddenly aren't responding to texts/calls/emails. It eliminates the possibility of them assuming things that might not be true at all, and it lets them know exactly why you need a little break.

Now, if *you* are the one receiving The Silent Treatment from a friend, instead of falling into the trap of assumptions, I would encourage you to reach out and simply say something like:

"I haven't heard from you in a while. I hope everything is Ok. If I've done something to upset you, please know you can tell me. We don't have to talk about it right now, but I'd rather know what the problem is instead of concluding something that might not be true. Your friendship means a lot to me, and I don't want a false assumption to cause more damage to our relationship."

Friendship Killers

Then the ball is in her court. If you still don't hear back from her, then you can know that you did what you could to "keep your side of the street clean," as some of my friends in the recovery world might say. It's good advice. We can't control other people, only ourselves. But hopefully, if your friendship is strong, it will mean a lot to her that you reached out and she'll respond in kind. Human beings are all flawed, and navigating relationships can be tricky at times, but The Silent Treatment never helps mend anything. So, please do what you can to avoid this "friendship killer."

* * *

Common Enemy Intimacy

One of my favorite books is called *Braving The Wilderness: The Quest for True Belonging and the Courage to Stand Alone* by Brené Brown. If you haven't heard of Brené, she is a very popular author, speaker and research professor that exploded onto the scene in 2010 with a Ted Talk about vulnerability. It has become the fourth most watched Ted Talk of all time, surpassing over 51 million views as I'm writing this. Clearly, the topic of vulnerability hit a nerve with many, many people. Since then, she has released other books, podcasts and even a Netflix special called, *"The Call to Courage."* She speaks and writes on many topics, including shame, empathy, bravery, trust, and perfectionism. Topics that deeply affect us all.

God and My Girlfriends

In *Braving The Wilderness,* Brown talks about the difference between belonging and fitting in. Everyone can figure out how to fit into a friendship circle if they really want to. All they have to do is pretend to like the same things, laugh at the same jokes, dress the same, worship the same, vote the same, enjoy the same hobbies, etc. Just become what *they* are and BOOM. . .you'll find yourself "fitting in" in no time! But the kind of true belonging that we all desire goes far beyond just being *liked* by people we admire or respect. We want to be truly *known* by our circle of friends. In order for this to happen, we must be willing to be authentic and vulnerable.

Are we risking getting hurt or being rejected when we approach our friendships with open hearts like this? Yes. No doubt about it. But what is the alternative? Do we remain in surface-level relationships with people that don't really know the *real* us? I don't believe that's what anyone is truly looking for.

One thing we all need to avoid in our friendships is something called "Common Enemy Intimacy," which is a closeness that is forged based on hating the same things, or even hating the same people. That really is *not* a healthy way to bond with someone or base a friendship on, but it happens way too often. Brown coined this phrase and talked about it at length in her book. Her definition is this:

"Common Enemy Intimacy is counterfeit connection and the opposite of true belonging. If the bond we share

Friendship Killers

with others is simply that we hate the same people, the intimacy we experience is often intense, immediately gratifying, and an easy way to discharge outrage and pain. It is not, however, fuel for real connection."[2]

We've all fallen prey to this. You know how it starts. Your new coworker makes a snarky statement about your boss that you can't stand and you suddenly feel a kinship to her. Next thing you know, you are making plans to go for drinks after work and you spend the entire time talking about this person that you both dislike. The "friendship" continues, based entirely on your shared dislike for the boss. Of course, as soon as you stop working together, you might find it's actually hard to continue the friendship now that you don't have this common bond of the same "enemy" in your lives. Sound familiar?

Look, we all love to find people with common interests, but healthy intimacy shouldn't be built on talking badly about others. Negativity cannot be the common ground that unites a friendship.

* * *

Distractions

I used to be so proud of the fact that I considered myself a great "multi-tasker." I could watch the morning news AND check my emails at the same time. I could drive my son to school AND listen to songs I needed to record in the studio later that day. I could cook dinner AND talk on the phone with my Mom. I can go on and on, but you get the message. I was always doing two things at once, and I thought that was a good thing. Now I don't think multi-tasking is such a great idea.

I've realized now that any relationship in my life sometimes deserves my undivided attention, and when I'm doing two things at once, I'm usually not focusing well on at least one of those things, if not both. For example, I remember accidentally hitting "reply all" to a few emails that I should NOT have "replied all" to—and it got me in a bit of hot water a couple of times! This happened because I was sending emails AND watching the "Deals and Steals" segment on *"Good Morning America"* at the same time. Bad move. I know that emails might not seem like a "relationship" to you, but any correspondence with another person is a type of relationship, and we should be paying attention to what we are saying (or typing) as much as we can.

And all those morning drives in the car with my son to school? Gosh, I look back and regret that we didn't spend those times in the car talking more. Instead, because I was often busy prepping for work during the drive, he would usually just put in his earbuds and listen to music, staring out the window. Man, I was a big dummy to waste those moments with him.

And now that my Mom has passed away, what I wouldn't

Friendship Killers

GIVE to have an undivided conversation with her, just listening to what was on her heart instead of half-listening while throwing some spaghetti in a pot for dinner.

I was expressing these regrets to my therapist one day, shedding tears on her couch for "what might have been," and she wisely told me that I needed to let myself off the hook.

"You were doing the best you could at the time, with the information you had, and at the emotional maturity level of which you were." Big sigh. She was right. It reminded me of a wonderful quote by Maya Angelou:

"Do the best you can until you know better. And when you know better, do better."[3]

Now I feel like I know better. I know that we should try and live in the moment, giving our attention to what is in front of us. I have learned that Love is PRESENCE. Giving someone our undivided attention is so very loving and it nurtures the relationship in a way nothing else will. It says, "YOU matter," and it says. "I'M listening,"—two critical parts of a healthy friendship.

This reminds me of another one of Maya's wonderful quotes:

"I've learned that people will forget what you said, people will forget what you did, but people will never forget how you made them feel."[4]

So, the next time you set aside time to spend with your girlfriend or girlfriends, try to avoid bringing distractions into that space together. Make them feel special. Put away the phone, leave behind the office drama, and ask your kids/husband to honor your time with your friends by handling all the household crises that might come up ("Where's the KETCHUP? Is there any clean laundry? The dog just threw up!")—and give that friend (or friends) your love and attention. Give her your presence. She'll never forget how you made her feel.

* * *

One Size Doesn't Fit All

Of course, every friendship is a little different and there are many more ways to damage a relationship besides the ones I've mentioned. However, I hope you can use these as a starting place towards learning things that will NOT nurture your friendships well. You can't approach every friendship exactly the same way because there is no such thing as "one size fits all" when it comes to relationships. This is actually a good thing! Who wants a friendship circle where every single person acts the same, looks the same, thinks the same, wants the same, needs the same. That would be bor-ing.

Nurturing each relationship takes intention. That's why when you offer your presence and truly pay attention, you'll learn what *this* friend needs from you in the

Friendship Killers

relationship. Then you can, in turn, be able to let her know what you need as well. *That* is a good practice for a healthy friendship.

Reflections

1. Do you struggle with constantly comparing yourself to your friends? How does that make you feel?

2. Do you ever feel like you are trying harder at maintaining friendships than your friends do? What can you do to change that?

3. How do you respond when a friend hurts your feelings? Do you back away and create distance without telling your friend why? If so, has that helped your friendships or hurt them?

4. How often do you find yourself involved in gossip? Are you the one who starts the gossip conversations, or do you just find yourself getting pulled into gossip by your friends? How can you work toward eliminating gossip in your relationships?

5. What changes can you make to be more present when you gather with friends?

CHAPTER EIGHT

Why Diversity Matters

"Diversity may be the hardest thing for a society to live with, and perhaps the most dangerous thing for a society to be without."— WILLIAM SLOANE COFFIN JR.[1]

LIKE I JUST MENTIONED at the end of the last chapter, no two friendships will work exactly the same. That is because each friend is a different person with different ideas, wants, and needs—and that is a wonderful thing. I can't stress enough the importance of diversity in our friendship circles. Most organizations that I see really thriving contain a diverse group in the infrastructure, holding it all together. Whether it's a business, a church, a non-profit, or just a circle of friends, the groups that have diversity seem to be stronger. Why? Well, because like Miranda Lambert sings, "It takes all kinds of kinds".[2]

Yes, it takes all kinds of people to make the world go 'round. Trust me when I say I am very grateful to have such a variety of people in my life. If I've said it once, I've said it a thousand times . . . we learn best from one another. Meaning, we trust the information we get from our close relationships, rather than from strangers. I can learn about so many different things from the experience of my friends. If I have a medical question, I'll call a friend who is in the medical field. If I have a cooking question, I'll call a friend who I know is a wonderful cook. If my dog is sick, I'll call a friend who works with animals. See where I'm going here? Yes, I could google the answers to some of these questions, but I trust the personal recommendation from a friend wayyyyy more than Mr. Google! When you have friends with a variety of skill sets and knowledge in differing areas, you'll be amazed at the support you find just a phone call away. It's awesome how that works! God makes us all unique with different passions and talents, and we can help each other walk through this life a little easier by sharing our knowledge and gifts with one another. Not only do we have unique gifts, but we have unique personalities too.

* * *

Personalities

A few years ago, I was introduced to the Enneagram, and it was life-changing. Not only did it help me learn so much about myself and the choices (both good and bad) that I

Why Diversity Matters

make each day, but I also learned a LOT about the loved ones around me. It helped me understand how differently we are all wired and that sometimes, when someone doesn't see things the same way I do, it's not because they are trying to be difficult or butt up against me. It's truly just because *they don't see things the same way I do.*

For example, after much study I found that I am an Enneagram 9, which is sometimes called "The Peacemaker." Now, some members of my family might laugh at that description of me, but yep, that's me. I'll do just about anything to have peace surrounding me, even if I have to scream at everyone to get it! I hate conflict with a passion. I hate it so much that I have spent much of my life just trying to *avoid* conflict, which doesn't always serve me well. Now that I understand that about myself, I'm learning how to actually *engage* in conflict in a healthy way, rather than avoid it, which never really solves anything.

Like I mentioned in Chapter Two, I've heard some people say they don't like personality tests because they "put me in a box," but that's not my experience with the Enneagram at all. It actually has helped me learn to get *out* of the box that I put myself in for years. And, it has strengthened my relationships as I now have a better understanding about what drives my loved ones and what makes them tick.

For example, my husband is an Enneagram 1, The Perfectionist/Reformer. His brain works very differently than mine, and that is a *good thing*. I'm not discounting either one of us, I'm just saying that we have different ways of approaching problem solving and, because of that, when one of us has hit a wall, usually the other one can come at the problem with a different perspective and help the other one see the solution. I can see the differences between us as a good thing. And, when we are in conflict about an issue, instead of feeling like he is being difficult and taking his inability to see things my way personally, I'm able to understand that I'm processing the situation like a 9 would, and he's processing it like a 1. It's not personal. It's just how we are wired.

That goes with friendships. Sometimes, even with your closest friends, you are going to see things very differently, and that's Ok. For instance, I am an unabashed Disney freak. Several years ago, one of my best friends and I found ourselves working together in Orlando, FL and she mentioned she had never been to Disneyworld.

"WH-AT??? WE GOTTA GO!!" I screamed.

Before she could even agree or disagree, I had passes bought and plans made for us to spend our day off at Disneyworld together. Truth be told, she wasn't one bit excited about this adventure I was planning for us, but she didn't quite have the heart to tell me. So, bless her heart, she woke up extra early, slammed down some coffee and got on the little Disney tram with me to experience her first day at the Magic Kingdom. We hadn't even made it through the entrance, and she was already grumbling about everything,

Why Diversity Matters

and she continued throughout the day —from the crowds ("these lines are soooo long"), to the heat, ("why didn't you tell me to bring my sunscreen. I'm going to burn!"), the price of the food, ("my boyfriend warned me everything was going to be expensive"). . .she even complained about the Jungle Cruise ("you mean there aren't REAL alligators? Is that all this is? Plastic fake jungle animals?") Without realizing it, she was stealing my "magic" in the Magic Kingdom, and by the end of the day I was ready to choke her. "What is WRONG with her?" I'm thinking to myself. Well, what was *wrong* with her is that I had drug her into a situation that she was never really interested in getting into in the first place. I just assumed because I loved it there, she would too. Now I find it humorous that I was so completely unaware of her misery, and yet because she loved me, she was trying as best she could to find what it was that I loved about the place. (I have since found out that Disney is quite polarizing. Either you love the place or hate it. Lesson learned!)

The bottom line is, we aren't all going to love the same things, because we all have different personalities—and THAT'S OK. We can still be good friends. And we *should* be friends with differing personalities. For instance, without my extroverted Enneagram 7 friends, I'd probably never get the nerve up to try exciting new things, choosing instead for my comfortable couch most days. I love how my bold Enneagram 8 friends will fight for things when I'm too shy to speak up. I love how my Enneagram 1 friends give me organizational tips when I'm just a big old unorganized mess most days. I could go on and on, but the bottom line is after understanding the different personality traits, I've learned to appreciate them ALL. and I make a conscious effort to keep them all in my circle of friends. It truly makes my circle complete.

* * *

Cultures, Religions and Skintones

My husband and I watched the mini-series *Unorthodox*[3] on Netflix recently. It's the award-winning mini-series about a girl who breaks away from an arranged marriage and the Hasidic Jewish culture in Brooklyn and flees to Germany. It really made an impact on me in many ways. . . but the main thing that I took away from it is that our upbringing and the culture in which we are raised plays a big part in who we eventually become.

I was two months old when I was adopted by a Christian couple who raised me in a Christian environment, but I could have easily been adopted into a different family who practiced a different religion—or no religion at all. If that had been the case, I'm sure that I would have become a very different human being than I am today. I'm not saying I would be better or worse. . .just very different is my guess. This reinforces my belief that we must start trying to understand those who are different than us a little better if we are ever going to fully love one another and avoid the "us vs them" mentality.

Why Diversity Matters

We ALL have preconceived biases and prejudices. In my experience, I find that most of them are rooted in an underlying fear. It's a fear that makes us feel our way of life might be threatened somehow, by people different from us, but usually that fear just comes from a lack of understanding one another.

I find when I take the time to listen to someone that I don't see eye to eye with, even if I still don't agree with their thinking or beliefs, I can at least find some compassion for them and a deeper understanding of how they came to believe what they believe. There is always a story behind the person—and a person behind the story. *Unorthodox* was a great reminder of that to me.

* * *

Arkadelphia, Arkansas—Population 10,123

Like I mentioned in "My Story" at the beginning of this book, I grew up in the small Arkansas town of Arkadelphia. It was and still is a lovely town and I feel lucky to have grown up in small-town America during simpler times. I was somewhat sheltered and felt safe from "outsiders"—no stranger danger!!—but looking back I see now how homogenous my upbringing was. My parent's friendship circles all looked very similar. Mostly white, southern, working middle class, church going, teetotalers. In recent years, I've become close with several black friends in my age group, and I am realizing that my version of "Mayberry" was very, *very,* different than theirs. Now I can clearly see that I was living in a very strong "white bubble" and had no idea how the black people in my little community were living or being treated. I had no idea, because I didn't have any close friends who weren't white. I honestly don't remember ever going into a home where a black person lived while I was in Arkadelphia. I'm not proud of that, but it's the truth.

I grew up in the 60's and 70's, so there was still much segregation in Arkansas communities back then. There were "black" churches, stores, restaurants etc, and "white" churches, stores, and restaurants . . . and you just didn't see those lines being crossed. In most public areas, you rarely saw intermingling.

Race relations started coming to a head in the 70's, and the tensions started rising in our town. Riots broke out in the high school, and many people were injured by being thrown through glass windows. Because of that, the school board decided that the answer was to build a new high school on the outskirts of town that had no windows. GREAT IDEA GUYS. So, when I entered high school, I went to school in a building that literally looked like a prison. No windows anywhere. Looking back, I can't *imagine* that it was good for any of us to spend all our days in windowless rooms, but that was what happened.

Of course, the windowless rooms didn't stop the racial

tensions from escalating. There were many days that we heard our vice-principal come over the loud speaker and instruct *"All the black students go to the cafeteria. All the white students go to the 'Little Theatre'."* (The "Little Theatre" was the name for our high school auditorium.) There we would gather and the faculty would make weak attempts at convincing us to "do better" at getting along with each other. Funny though, what I remember is that they basically just instructed us to try and *avoid* one another as much as possible.

"Don't bother each other," they said.

Not bothering each other isn't the same as learning to understand one another. There were never any REAL skills taught to us about how to learn unification and improve race relations. It was more about learning to "tolerate" one another. The thought of hanging out with each other and becoming actual friends was never really encouraged. Now, please understand, I'm not trying to portray anyone here as good or bad, right or wrong. If it feels like I'm painting with broad strokes, that's not my intention. It was just the state of the times and the state of our culture.

I do believe we have made strides in our country, strides past some of the linear thinking that leads to irrational bias; however, it seems that in recent years we have taken a few steps backward. Not just racially either. The teams have been chosen:

God and My Girlfriends

Women vs Men.

Rich vs Poor.

North vs South.

Heterosexuals vs Homosexuals.

Protestants vs Catholics.

Christians vs Muslims.

Americans vs THE REST OF THE WORLD.

America used to have pride in its diverse roots; however, somewhere along the way, we lost that pride and started picking teams. If you weren't on our team then you became our rival. Rivals eventually became enemies, and that mentality has gotten us in a HEAP of trouble as a country and also in many of our Christian communities.

One of the chapters from the book, *I Think You're Wrong (But I'm Listening)* by Sarah Stewart Holland and Beth Silvers is titled "Take off your Jerseys." What that means is we have to stop separating ourselves into teams, huddling up with those who only look, act and think like us and start reaching out across tribal lines. We can't approach life like a sporting event. If we do, we miss out on the richness and diversity that God created when He created the WHOLE world.

So how do we combat the unhealthy and irrational fear of people who are different from us?

Why Diversity Matters

We start up close and personal. We start with our own *friendships*.

* * *

What does your girlfriend community look like? How diverse is your "team"?

Are you in community or friendships with women who look different, live differently, or have experienced life differently than you have? I am here to say that I believe that it is immensely important! It is the way God intended it.

Matthew 28:19 tells us to make disciples of ALL nations. If we are to make disciples of all nations, then we are to cultivate *friendships* of all nations.

James 2 tells us to have no partiality, even among those who dress differently than we do. This passage describes a class system and how we are not to divide people as "haves" and "have-nots." "*You shall love your neighbor as yourself,*" he tells us. Like I mentioned in the introduction to this book, our "neighbor" is simply "others"—including those who we see as different from us.

I have had so many times in my life where women who have gone before me, or have had totally different experiences than me, have been able to show me a whole new perspective on life.

God and My Girlfriends

Friends who are older have more words of wisdom.

Friends with different skin tones have different racial and cultural experiences.

And *friends who are younger* can speak truth into us from the younger generation's perspective. We know at the later stages in life how important it is to stay relevant and to continue to learn and grow in order to not be left behind! We don't want to be left behind, ladies!

Community comes from all angles. Refusing to be open to other experiences and perspectives is so very limiting and unhealthy. It creates an echo chamber that gives us a false sense of the world, making us believe that all the "good" people are like *us*. . .when the truth might be very, very different. Taking time to cultivate diversity in your friendship circles will add a beautiful and unexpected richness to your life. Trust me on this!

* * *

Pop Quiz Time!

When I speak at women's events, I like to ask those in attendance to assess the current amount of diversity in their friendship circles. I start by asking them to fill out a questionnaire that looks something like this:

Name one friend who you feel truly knows you:

Why Diversity Matters

Name one friend you would like to be closer to:

Name one friend who makes you laugh:

Name one friend who holds you accountable:

Name the friend who you've known the longest and how many years you've been friends:

Name your newest friend and how you met:

Name one friend who is a different religion than you are:

Name one friend who is a different skin tone than you are:

Name one friend who is a different political persuasion than you are:

Name one friend who has a different sexual preference than you do:

Name one friend who isn't from America:

Name one friend who is at least 10 years older than you are:

Name one friend who is at least 10 years younger than you are:

Truthfully, most people struggle with filling in every slot. We need older friends, younger friends, funny friends, truthful friends, longtime friends, and new friends. We need friends of different cultures, religions, backgrounds, skintones. We truly *need* all these friends to make a fully round circle of friends and not one long echo chamber.

I was taking a walk in our neighborhood recently and noticed this sign in front of a neighbor's house:

"No importa de dónde eres, estamos contentos que seas nuestro vecino.

No matter where you are from, we're glad you're our neighbor.

ال يهم اين و لددتم، و لكننا سعداء انكم جيركم انا"

It was written in Spanish, English and Arabic.[4] I thought it was so beautiful and loving and welcoming. Can you imagine how scary it must be to come into a different country and try to start a new life? It reminded me that we shouldn't have to look too far to find a friend. If we are searching for friendships and we don't even know our next door neighbors, we are probably missing out on a wonderful opportunity. We are called to be the hands and feet of Jesus, and what better place to start than those in closest proximity to us. Don't be afraid to reach out to those around you. Even if . . . no, *especially if* they are different from you. Embrace the richness of diversity in friendships!

Why Diversity Matters

So why is "diversity in friendships" part of this book? Because I feel strongly that:

1. It is what God wants for us

2. We learn so much from others and can have a better understanding of the world we live in

3. It helps us to grow in Christ.

God created the human race and that includes people of all skin tones. Not only in America, but in the whole world. As we are willing to put ourselves out there and create relationships with women who don't look like us, act like us, think like us etc., then we will learn more about God's kingdom and how to serve it. We will learn about other women's stories, experiences, struggles, and celebrations. We will learn how to share in a love that transcends all of these things. We will be more like Jesus.

Reflections

1. Think about your friendship circles. Do you find diversity in them? If not, what might be the reason behind that?

2. Have you taken any personality tests, like the Enneagram? If so, have you found them helpful? What did you learn about yourself?

3. Have you ever thought about how the culture you grew up in might limit your understanding of the rest of the world? How could you break out of that mold?

4. Do you find yourself uncomfortable around people who are very different from you? What do you think is the root of that?

Why Diversity Matters

5. What's one thing you could do to add diversity in your friendships?

CHAPTER NINE

Sometimes Ya Gotta Fight!

"Whenever you're in conflict with someone, there is one difference between damaging your relationship and deepening it. That factor is attitude."—WILLIAM JAMES [1]

SEVERAL YEARS AGO, I found myself at odds with one of my oldest and dearest friends. For the sake of anonymity, let's call her "Shelly." She and I have been close friends for over 25 years. We met after we had both moved to Nashville, Tennessee to pursue the music business, and we ended up being in the same band for a hot minute. Shelly and I are probably one of those friendships that make some people who go "Huh??"—We are so *very* different.

First off, Shelly grew up in the New Jersey/NYC area, and I grew up in southwest Arkansas. I'm sure when she left New Jersey she thought she was downsizing to a smaller town, and when I moved to Nashville, I was terrified of moving to the BIG CITY!! I'm not kidding when I say that, when we first met, we were pretty much complete opposites. She was a hard-edged Jersey girl, agnostic, who used the "F" word like it was a typical adjective, and I was a sheltered, Christian country girl, who said "Bless her heart" every time Shelly used the "F" word. HA! Seriously, HOW DID WE BECOME FRIENDS? But we sure did!

I was immediately drawn to all her attributes that I felt I lacked. I admired her for the confidence she seemed to radiate—something I had always struggled with. She was gorgeous with flaming red hair. She played the heck out of a guitar, sang like Bonnie Raitt, and was just so dang COOL. I was in awe of my new friend. Soon after we met, we became bandmates and found ourselves spending a lot of time together. Our conversations eventually went beyond just work and got a bit more personal. At the time, I was still deeply steeped in evangelical Christianity, so one day after band rehearsal, I got up my nerve and invited her and her boyfriend to come visit my church.

"Hey, I'm singing the solo at church this weekend if you'd like to come!"

I remember an awkward moment of silence as they glanced at each other, both processing what I'd just said, and then she sweetly said to me with a smile, *"Ummm. thanks. We will think about it and let you know."* What I didn't know at the time was that she was Agnostic and he was Jewish!

Sometimes Ya Gotta Fight!

Whoa Lawd . . . I'm laughing just typing this memory out! I was seriously SO naive!! I thought everyone around me was a Christian!

But this awkward moment turned into the beginning of how I knew I could trust this person. Because sure enough, that next Sunday morning, as I stood up on stage singing with the worship team, I saw Shelly and her beau gingerly walking into the back door of the auditorium. They looked a little out of sorts and overwhelmed as the over-eager welcome volunteers shoved coffee, donuts and church bulletins into their hands. I gave them a big wave from the stage like, "HI! YOU'RE HERE!!! SO COOL!" and she gave me a big smile of support while simultaneously shooting me a look that said, "Yeah, I'm here, but don't ever ask me to come to this crazy place again!!" Ha.

Funny enough, she actually DID come again. . .and again . . . and again.

I'll never forget the day I hiked up to a waterfall where I saw Shelly get baptized in a mountain stream one glorious Saturday morning.

Over the years, I've watched her grow to love Jesus in the most beautiful way. While I may have had a small part in introducing her to Christ, she has taught me so much through the years about what it means to love others as a Jesus follower, and I'm so grateful for that.

God and My Girlfriends

Fast forward 20 years. We have been through *a lot* together by this time—standing by each other's side during all of life's big moments. We both cried together as we buried our parents—even singing at each other's father's funerals. She has cheered on my kids at their school functions as if they were her own. We have championed each other through our divorces, and encouraged each other to open our hearts to new love again. We were as close as friends could be. . .and yet, because of a series of circumstances, we found ourselves at a bad place in our friendship. Suddenly we were dealing with hurt feelings and distrust—and we really weren't sure if we could move forward.

I think we both had moments where we thought, "Well, we've been friends for 25 years and that was a good run, but MAN, she's on my LAST NERVE so I think it's probably just time to call it a day and move on." But you know what? We didn't. THANK GOD we didn't.

You know what we did instead? We actually went to counseling together. Yep, like an old married couple, we went to couples therapy! I remember going to her house and sitting down across from each other at her dining room table. We stared at each other with sad eyes that seemed to say, "*Now what?*" Since we both had the same therapist at the time, (the amazing Trish Sanders, who sadly passed away in 2019) I said:

"*What if we made an appointment to see Trish together? Do you think that would help us move forward in a healthy way?*"

Sometimes Ya Gotta Fight!

Now, I gotta say, I was TERRIFIED when I asked Shelly that question. What would I do if she refused? Would that mean that our friendship was over? Thankfully, she said, "Yeah, I'll do that." And we made an appointment right then and there.

Months later, after we were in a better place, I remember asking Shelly:

"Did you think that going to Trish was helpful for us?"

Her reply: *"Honestly, I don't really know. But just the fact that our friendship meant enough to you to ask me to go to therapy with you. Well, that in itself was huge for me."*

I laughed and said, *"You know what? I felt the same! Just the fact that you were willing to go with me showed me that you loved me and were willing to fight for our friendship."*

Friendships aren't always easy—and just like with any other relationship, sometimes we have to fight for them. I'll always be grateful that Shelly chose to fight for us.

* * *

Fighting Together

Now, when I say "fight," I hope you know I'm not using that word in a way that means you should fight *with* your friend. When I say "Sometimes, ya gotta fight!"—I'm talking about fighting *for* your friendship. Fighting to keep the relationship healthy and positive for both of you. All relationships have their ups and downs, but it takes intentional commitment for a friendship to last. There really is nothing more precious than an old friend.

Several years ago, Dolly Parton and Kenny Rogers recorded a song titled, "You Can't Make Old Friends."[2] I love these lyrics:

What will I do when you are gone?
Who's gonna tell me the truth?
Who's gonna finish the stories I start
The way you always do?

When somebody knocks at the door
Someone new walks in
I will smile and shake their hands
But you can't make old friends

You can't make old friends
Can't make old friends
It was you and me, since way back when
But you can't make old friends

How will I sing when you are gone?
'Cause it won't sound the same
Who will join in on those harmony parts
When I call your name?

Sometimes Ya Gotta Fight!

When Saint Peter opens the gate
And you come walking in
I will be there just waiting for you
'Cause you can't make old friends
You can't make old friends

It truly is worth it to fight for those long-term relationships. Several years ago, my husband and I hit a little hard patch in our marriage. I had been touring almost non-stop for several months and we found ourselves slowly drifting apart. Luckily, we both realized the distance that had formed between us and decided together to go to counseling. (Again, we got Trish on the phone. I'm not kidding when I say that her guidance saved many of my relationships. God bless her. A good therapist is worth their weight in GOLD.) Anyway, I'll never forget something my husband said to me the morning of our big discussion about the state of our relationship. He said:

"You know honey, a relationship is like a flower. There are two ways to kill it. You can either go outside and stomp on it until it's dead. Or, you can simply stop watering it. Either way, it's going to die."[3]

WHOA. Pretty profound for a small-town Michigan boy, huh? But his words struck me deeply. He was so right. While neither of us had done anything really harmful to our relationship (no affairs, no deceit, no abuse etc.)—we simply had not been watering it.

After a few sessions with Trish, we were back on track, even better than ever. I'll take this moment to once again reiterate how valuable good therapy can be—for you and for all your relationships. Everyone should have a good therapist on speed dial!

Just remember that friendships take watering too, especially the long-term relationships that we can sometimes take for granted. One day, you just seem to wake up and don't feel close anymore.

Don't let that happen.

If you find a friend who has stuck with you through the years, recognize the loyalty and value of that kind of friend. . .and *fight for her.*

Reflections

1. Do you have a friend who seems to be your "opposite"? What are some of the things that drew you to her? Do you still appreciate those things today? If not, why?

Sometimes Ya Gotta Fight!

2. How do you choose to handle conflict with a friend? Does your method usually end up mending the conflict? If not, what is one thing you can do to choose a healthier means of conflict management?

3. How can having friends with different strengths than ours be a good thing in our lives?

4. How do you feel about therapy? If you haven't ever tried it, what is holding you back?

5. What is the name of your oldest friend? (Not by age, but by length of friendship) What does that relationship mean to you now? What's one thing you can do to nurture that relationship better?

CHAPTER TEN

Friendship in the Bible

"A friend loves at all times, and a sister is born for adversity."—(Proverbs 17:17)

THERE IS SO MUCH to be learned about friendship from the Bible. There are beautiful passages that speak to the value of friendship, and many stories of committed friends and their adventures together. However, the Bible also shows examples of the messiness of friendships: Betrayals. Separations. Arguments. Break-ups. Disillusionments. Fear of Abandonment.—It's all in there. The good, the bad, the joys, the heartbreaks.

We also see that it's sometimes in these more difficult relationships that we grow and become stronger in character. We become better at understanding each other. We become wiser, more patient, and more in-tune with those around us.

God and My Girlfriends

Here are a few examples of great friendships in the Bible. Yes, some are friendships among men, but we can learn from their relationships too.

1. **Jonathan and David**—you can find their story written in 1 Samuel. There is no doubt that they had a deep, abiding friendship. So strong, that after Jonathan died, David took in Jonathan's son as his own. But the most interesting part about their friendship is how unlikely it was. Jonathan was King Saul's eldest son. He was in line to be the next King after his father. But along came David, impressing Saul with his slaying of the Philistines and rising up in the ranks. Many people in Jonathan's shoes might have felt envy, suspicion, and possibly even fear that David was going to take away what was Jonathan's rightful inheritance. But instead, the Bible says that, *"the soul of Jonathan was knit to the soul of David, and Jonathan loved him as his own soul."*[1] So, these two actually developed an unlikely friendship, choosing relationship, companionship and collaboration over competition. What a powerful story!

2. **Moses and Aaron**—these two are the perfect example of friends using their unique abilities and strengths to accomplish something great together. Actually, there is another added element to their friendship. Moses and Aaron were also brothers. In Exodus, we read the story of God calling Moses to lead the Israelites out of bondage in Egypt and into the Promised Land. But Moses was a reluctant leader because he had a speech impediment. The

Friendship in the Bible

Bible doesn't exactly say what Moses' problem was—many think he had a stutter—but nevertheless, he was afraid to speak in public because of it. So, God appointed Aaron as his speaker and supporter, and together they had a fruitful partnership. The big "take aways" for me in this story are that it's good to have friends with different skill sets than you. And also, that you might find a deep and valuable friendship right within your own family.

3. ***Paul, Barnabus and Mark***—The friendship of these three men reminds us that conflict can arise, but we shouldn't be too hasty in counting someone out as a friend. In Acts 15, we see where Paul and Barnabus get into a disagreement on whether or not to let Mark continue working with them. Paul is ready to cut ties with Mark, because apparently Mark had flaked out on them in Pamphylia, leaving them to finish the work there alone. I mean, you can't really blame Paul for being hesitant to trust the guy again. We've all had "that flaky friend." But Barnabus went to bat for Mark, feeling that he deserved a second chance.

Because Paul and Barnabus couldn't come to an agreement, they went their separate ways. Paul ended up taking another friend, Silas with him to Syria and Barnabus took Mark with him to Cyprus. Now if great leaders of our faith like Paul and Barnabus couldn't get along and parted ways, then that just shows us that friendships are not always smooth sailing.

The good news is that they all eventually came back together, working towards the same goal of strengthening God's Kingdom. In 2 Timothy, Paul now speaks of Mark highly. In his letter to Timothy, he says, *"Do your best to come to me quickly. Get Mark and bring him with you, because he is helpful to me in my ministry."*² Sounds to me like all is healed and forgiven! And young Mark even ended up writing one of our four gospels. So, although he might have had a rocky start, Mark ended up doing great things for God. Learning to give one another second chances is a key to long-lasting friendships.

4. **Ruth and Naomi**—this friendship shows us the value of loyalty and self-sacrifice. Ruth and Naomi start out bonded as family because young Ruth marries one of Naomi's sons. But due to a series of unfortunate events, Naomi loses everything. Her husband dies and then both of her sons die as well. In those days, a woman without a husband or sons was destitute. Women couldn't own property for themselves. Widows had to depend on friends and strangers to offer them food or shelter. Naomi told both of her daughters-in-law to leave her and go find new husbands while they were still young enough to have families of their own. Ruth refused to leave Naomi. Both women showed sacrificial love for one another in that moment. They both wanted what was best for the other and were willing to go to great extremes to make sure the other was cared for. You can read the whole story in the Old Testament book of *Ruth*. It is a beautiful story and reminds us that loyalty is an important aspect of deep, authentic friendship.

Friendship in the Bible

* * *

My Favorite Verses

There are so many Bible verses that speak about friendship that there have been entire books written just on those passages. For now, I'm just going to highlight a few of my absolute favorites, which all come from the book of Proverbs. I want to start out with a verse that inspired me as I began to imagine what *God And My Girlfriends Ministries* might look like.

* * *

"A sweet friendship refreshes the soul"
—PROVERBS 27:9

The Value of Friendship: There are actually many different translations of this verse that I love. Another one says, *"The heartfelt counsel of a friend is as sweet as perfume and incense."*[3] The Bible is telling us the value of friendship. I swear, there is just nothing like gathering around a table and breaking bread with a group of people you love— and that you know love you back. It's life-giving. It truly "refreshes the soul." Having wise friends who can counsel you through those difficult times in life? Well, that is just simply invaluable. Just like those Mastercard commercials that break-down the value of things, a friend who gives good advice is priceless! Because I have been blessed with wonderful friendships in my life, I felt God calling me to help others find the blessings of good, authentic friendships. And Proverbs 27:9 was definitely part of my inspiration as we began GAMG Ministries.

* * *

> *"Walk with the wise and become wise, for a companion of fools suffers harm."*
> —PROVERBS 13:20

How to Choose Your Friends: We talked in Chapter Six about the importance of choosing our friends, and this verse in Proverbs speaks to that. Author and poet, C.J. Heck talks about how we are all influenced greatly by everything that surrounds us.

"We are all products of our environment; every person we meet, every new experience or adventure, every book we read, touches and changes us, making us the unique being we are." [4]

This is so true—including the friends we choose. They will shape us and affect our lives in many, many ways. There are other quotes that I'm sure you've heard through the years like, *"Show me your friends and I'll show you your future."* Or, *"You are the average of the 5 people closest to you."* I'm not sure where those quotes originated from, but you get the idea. Following the wisdom from Proverbs 13:20 is advice that has been backed up for years by study after study. It's solid advice. Make sure you choose your friends wisely.

Friendship in the Bible

* * *

"A friend loves at all times, and a sister is born for times of adversity."—PROVERBS 17:17

How to be a good friend: It's easy to love someone when everything is going great for them. When they are happy, successful and full of joy, we *love* hanging out with them and treasure their influence and companionship. But what about those friends who are living through difficult times and aren't happy and joyful to be around right now. Do we find ourselves pulling away from them? Do we struggle with friends who aren't capable of giving back to us? Are we hesitant to call and check up on friends who are going through low times?

I had a friend tell me one time that her divorce was one of the most painful times in her life, and not just because her marriage was ending. Much of the pain came from the silence of her friends. She said she felt like a leper, with many of her friends suddenly avoiding her calls or being too busy to get together for dinner anymore. I think many times the silence stems from just not knowing what to say to our friends who are hurting. No matter what painful situation they are living through—whether it's grieving the death of a loved one, a job loss, general depression, a romantic break-up, etc., we must find ways to support and help them through it. Sometimes it just means "being there." We might not solve their problems, but we can make sure they know that they are not alone.

God and My Girlfriends

I've had friends go silent on me before—and it's awful. Many years ago I got fired from my job, and all the "friends" I worked with distanced themselves from me seemingly overnight. Just like my girlfriend who told me that losing friendships after her divorce was almost worse than the divorce itself, it was the loss of relationships that hurt me worse than losing the job. It's times like that when we really find out who our true friends are. So for that, we can be thankful.

We must learn how to love our friends well, not just in good times, but in the bad. It's a critical part of real, authentic relationship. It won't be easy sometimes, but that's what a true friend does.

* * *

*"As Iron sharpens iron, so
one person sharpens another"*
—Proverbs 27:17

Better Together: Some people read this passage and think that the lesson here is simply that we need each other and we are better together—which is very true. But, by using the metaphor of *iron* sharpening *iron,* there is another layer to this verse that many overlook.

Have you ever seen the actual process of iron sharpening iron? When iron is pounded against iron for sharpening and shaping, it creates friction. It gets hot. Sparks may

Friendship in the Bible

even fly. Sometimes we think of relationships in Christ-centered community as always being smooth and without conflict, always gracious and loving, never needing apologies, never hurting each other's feelings. Friends, I think all of us know that relationships are messy and most certainly will have friction at times, even among the closest of friends. That's ok. That friction is sometimes needed. We shouldn't fear that aspect of community. That is how we can sharpen one another.

Also, when iron sharpens iron, both pieces change—the sharpener *and* the one being sharpened. As long as we work on handling conflict in healthy ways—offering genuine apologies, reconciling when we don't agree, listening to one other, learning from each other and being humble in our differences, then both pieces of iron (or friends) come out re-shaped and sharper for it. *That* is when we find authentic community that allows us to become stronger, together.

Like I said, there are many verses in the Bible that give us advice on friendship—wisdom that has held up for thousands of years. It is simply *the* source of some of the best examples of friendship that we can find, even in our culture today. It tells us what to look for in a friend, and also how to be a great friend. Yes, there are hundreds of books out there on the shelves (including this one) that will try to offer you good relational advice. But I hope you'll always use The Bible as your number one resource for advice on friendships and for all relationships. It will never lead you astray.

Reflections

1. What is your favorite bible verse about friendship? Why does it resonate with you?

2. What is your favorite friendship story in the Bible? Do you have a friendship that has similar qualities?

3. Why do you think there is so much emphasis on friendships in the Bible?

Friendship in the Bible

4. Do you feel there is a spiritual component to your friendships? What does that look like?

5. Why do you think God wants us to have friends?

Part Three: GOD
The Great Connection

*"Blessed is she who has believed that
the Lord would fulfill his promises to her."*
—LUKE 1:45

CHAPTER ELEVEN

What Do I Think About God?

> *"What comes into our minds when we think about God is the most important thing about us."*
> — A.W. Tozer[1]

AS I EXPLAINED in my story, I started thinking about God from an early age, and I am so thankful to my God-loving parents for introducing me to our Creator during my early childhood. Understanding that there was an all-knowing God up in heaven who created me and everything around me with love, care and concern made me feel special, loved, and protected. I could sing "Jesus loves the little children" with all the faith in the world that he indeed did and *does*.

But then as I grew older and life started happening, things beyond my control...scary, hurtful, confusing things... it was easy to start wondering where God was in all of the mess. Why were awful things happening? Had God turned his back on me? Had I made too many mistakes for God to intervene now and fix my circumstances? WHAT WAS GOING ON?

My "rock-bottom" moment with my faith happened after my first divorce. I mentioned in my story that I grew up Southern Baptist but started attending a Church of Christ during my first marriage because that was my husband's religious affiliation at the time. Right after we got married, we attended a small Church of Christ in Nashville, Arkansas where we lived in our first year of marriage. It was filled with loving people but looking back I can see they were following a very legalistic religion that didn't give much room for God's grace. You followed the rules as they taught them or you risked going to hell. I did my very best to learn how to become a good Christian wife and mother under the guidance of the women in that church, but I was so caught up in all that comes with a brand new baby, which includes NO SLEEP, that most of it was just a blur. It was all I could do to get through each day, meeting the needs of my new baby and trying to learn how to be a wife. I was completely overwhelmed.

In 1984, we moved to Nashville, Tennessee so that my then-husband could pursue a career in the music business. We had a one-year-old baby at the time, so although I yearned to pursue a career in music too, it wasn't an option. Women stayed home, raised their children and supported their husbands. Period. I tried to be happy and content, but there was a deep gnawing of guilt in my gut that I couldn't shake. I'll never forget the day we told my future mother-in-law that I was pregnant (remember, we were unmarried at the time). Her words are seared into my mind:

"Well, you've ruined your lives. You had so much promise Marcia, and now you'll have to give up all your dreams."

Before I go any further, I want to clarify that my now ex-Mother-in-law isn't a mean person. She's a loving person who was scared and sad for her son at the time. In her disappointment, she said some harsh things. We've all done it, so I do not in any way intend to vilify her. Nevertheless, those words stuck with me for years. It became part of the story I told myself about who I was. I had made a horrible decision to have sex outside of marriage and now I'm being punished for it . . . forever. My childhood vision of a loving, grace-filled God had now shifted to a God who was mad at me for sinning and was set out to make sure I knew how disappointed he was in me.

My religious life now consisted of getting up every Sunday morning, dressing in my best Sunday clothes, dropping off my infant in the church nursery and then sitting through a church service that usually made me feel even worse about myself, before going home and crying my eyes out. It was my Sunday ritual for years. My husband was traveling 250 days a year, pursuing his music dreams, playing guitar on the road with famous country singers, and I felt entirely alone. He wasn't around, I barely knew anyone in Nashville, so I had few friends, and worst of all, God was "too mad" at me to offer me any comfort. It was a dark time. Thank goodness for my baby boy who was the light of my world and truly got me through each day. He was my hope. He was my reason for getting up each morning and trying to get it right . . . but God felt so very far away, and I didn't know how to find my way back to him.

As our marriage deteriorated, things went from bad to worse. I had stopped going to church altogether because I just couldn't sit through the spiritual "beat downs" I was experiencing each Sunday morning. After our divorce, a whole new level of guilt settled in on me as I realized more and more bad choices had wrecked my world. I even contemplated suicide. But I had been taught that suicide was the "unforgivable sin" that the Bible talks about (which I do not believe anymore). I surely didn't want to end up in hell, so I kept living in my own "hell on earth" trying to sort out what I could possibly do to make things better. In a desperate attempt to try and get God's help, I ran to the nearest Church of Christ that I could find and started attending church again. Maybe if I followed all the "rules" this time, God would forgive me and help me get my life back on track. I jumped back in whole-heartedly and did everything I thought I was supposed to do; however, that's when the final straw came. When I tried to join the church, I was rejected. Why? They said I couldn't become a member of their church because I was divorced.

What Do I Think About God?

WHAT????

"*I don't understand,*" I said, clearly confused.

They explained that while I was welcome to attend the church, I couldn't actually JOIN the church because they didn't allow divorced people to become members.

"*What am I supposed to do now?*" I asked.

"*Go back to your husband and make things right with him.*"

I was incredulous, "*But my husband is married to someone else now.*" I explained, with a bit of panic starting to rise up in my gut.

"*Well,*" they said, "*Then that's going to be on him to explain to God on judgment day.*"

I couldn't believe it. I walked out of that church and sat in my car in their parking lot sobbing my eyes out. The words of my now former mother-in-law steering straight into my heart once again, "*You've ruined your life Marcia. You had so much promise but . . .*" I remember staring up at the sky and saying, "Okay, God. I finally get it. I've screwed up too much and you're done with me, so I'm done with you too. See ya." I started my car, drove off that church property and didn't look back for several years. Today, my heart breaks for that girl. She was broken and went to the church for healing, yet came out feeling even worse! How messed up was that?? She mistook the rejection and judgment from humans as a rejection and judgment from God. So what she thought about God at that moment was that she had gone too far, messed up too much, and there was no going back. She thought God had given up on her and that he didn't love her anymore. That belief greatly affected the way she lived her life over the next few years. That belief affected all the choices she made, from the people she chose to hang out with, the substances she chose to put in her body, and the way she thought about herself. She wasn't good to herself because deep down, she believed if God had given up on her, then why should she believe in herself either.

I'm so grateful that God found a way to show me how wrong I was about him. It certainly didn't happen overnight, but he surely sent a few angels along my path to show me that he was still loving me as much as he ever had; that he was watching over me in ways I couldn't even have imagined; and that he was still right there beside me, ready to shower me with goodness and truth and guidance . . . and love. When I started believing all that, and I mean TRULY started believing it . . . everything changed.

One of my favorite people to follow on twitter is writer and speaker, Beth Moore. I swear, it's worth staying on twitter just for her daily inspiration. Her humor is on point too. One of my recent favorites from her was this:

What Do I Think About God?

> **"God's not one whit changed by what we believe about him. But what we believe about him dramatically changes us."[2]**

Yes, what we think about God is THE most important thing in life because it changes us. It shapes the way we view everything and everyone around us, including ourselves. Our view of God will ultimately be what determines what our future paths look like. So if you aren't happy with your current situation and want to see real change in your life, start with getting to know God, your Creator.

God should be the cornerstone on which all other relationships are built. He is the firmest of foundations, and we all need a solid rock upon which to stand.

Reflections

1. What are the first adjectives you think about when you think of God? Are they positive words, like "loving," "merciful," "unwavering," "faithful," or "gracious"? Or are they negative words, like "judgmental," "harsh," "unforgiving"?

2. Look up Psalm 145:17, Exodus 34: 6-7, Malachi 3:6, James 1:17, 1 Samuel 2:2, Acts 17:27-28 and 1 John 4:8. What are some of the attributes of God that you can find in these verses?

3. In my story, there was a time I mistook the rejection of humans for a rejection from God. What does Deuteronomy 31:6 say about God's loyalty to you?

4. The Bible says that we can never go too far for God to still reach us. Read Psalm 139: 7 -10. How does that make you feel?

5. We can't love someone we don't know. What is one way you can start getting to know God better?

CHAPTER TWELVE

Soul Care

> *"The soul seeks God with its whole being. Because it is desperate to be whole, the soul is God-smitten and God-crazy and God-obsessed. My mind may be obsessed with idols; my will may be enslaved to habits; my body may be consumed with appetites. But my soul will never find rest until it rests in God."* — J. Ortberg[1]

HAVE YOU EVER NOTICED that when writers refer to a tragic event where many people died at once, they often talk about how many souls were lost? For instance, when you read about how many died during the sinking of the Titanic, you will see that most reports say, *"More than 1,500 souls were lost at sea."* They don't say that 1,500 *bodies* were lost at sea. They say *souls*. That's a good reminder that we humans don't *have* a soul. We *have* a body—but we ARE a soul.

. . . and our souls need care. Spiritual care.

Making our relationship with God our main priority will give us confidence in our relationships with others, and with ourselves. That's why it's so important that we start with getting our spiritual life in a good place, first and foremost.

How do we find ways to do that? Well, let's start at the beginning.

* * *

First Things First

Do you have a morning routine? Most women I speak with talk about certain things they do on a regular basis to kick-start their mornings. Things like drinking coffee (duh!), jumping in a hot shower, watching a morning show for news/weather, stretching/exercise, meditation and eating breakfast. One girl I know says she is so NOT a "morning person" that she does most of her routine at night. She showers, lays out what she is going to wear the next day, styles her hair and then puts on a sleeping cap. That way she can just get up each morning, brush her teeth, slip on her pre-planned outfit, put on a bit of makeup and head right out the door. Whatever works for ya, girlfriend! But most of us need a little more of a morning routine to get us going.

I have found that prayer, meditation, and devotion time is truly valuable in our morning routines. Yes, it means setting your alarm clocks a little earlier, but just get yourself into bed earlier at night and you will be OK. Trust me. This is worth the effort.

Many of you are familiar with Matthew 6:33. It says:

"But seek first His Kingdom and His righteousness, and all these things will be given to you as well."

That was always interpreted to me as meaning if you put God's will first in your life, all your other needs will be met. And that is a lovely interpretation. *The Message* version of that verse puts it this way:

"Steep your life in God-reality, God-initiative, God-provisions. Don't worry about missing out. You'll find all your everyday human concerns will be met."[2]

Doesn't that feel reassuring? In other words, when we worry about the things that God worries about, he'll make sure we are taken care of. Honestly, that is an amazing goal, but not always easy to do.

Kathie Lee Gifford was being interviewed recently, and I heard her explain a little twist to that verse. She said when she was praying over Matthew 6 one day, she felt God nudge her toward another meaning. Maybe, he meant for us to seek him *first each day* too—to start each and every day in prayer, bible study and devotion. That way, he can set our hearts and minds right, ready to handle whatever the day brings, in the way God wants us to. THAT is a truly tangible way of living out Matthew 6:33.

* * *

Getting Started

Everyone has different ways to approach morning time with God, but if you are struggling with how to start with this, let me give you just a few tips that have been helpful to me.

1. Find a comfortable and consistent space. One of my favorite books on prayer is by Diane Moody titled *Confessions of a Prayer Slacker.* As soon as I saw it, I knew I had found a kindred spirit in Diane! One of her suggestions was to find a special place that you go to each time you want to pray. So, when I am at home, I have a "prayer chair" in my sunroom that I settle into each morning. My family knows not to bother me when I'm in that chair unless something is on fire! But seriously, they do know that giving me that space in the morning to connect with God will make me a much better wife and mother, so they honor my time there. If I'm traveling for work and in a hotel or other housing, well, I just find a comfortable spot to start the day communing with God. Sometimes I'm crammed in my bunk on the bus, but I still make it work! I have friends who choose to have their morning time outside, weather permitting. Some like small enclosed spaces.

One friend I know has a "prayer closet" where she goes in the dark and prays/meditates. Another friend walks in the woods outside her country home each morning for her God connection time. There is no right or wrong here. Whatever gives you the "permission" to check out of the worldly distractions so that you can have time alone with God.

2. **Set a timer.** I know this might sound weird, but it can truly be helpful in relaxing and letting you shut out worries of getting so lost in study/prayer that you lose track of time and find yourself late for work, an appointment, or waking up the kids for school. Timers are your friend!

3. ***Avoid any/all technology if possible.*** Sometimes I use my phone, tablet or computer to look up Bible translations, research scripture, read devotionals. Technology is great for that, but make sure you put your electronics on airplane mode. There is nothing more distracting than constantly getting notifications. It takes your focus away from being in the moment with God. Seriously, it's a strong woman who can be in the middle of a bible study and ignore a notification that shows up on her screen that says something like, "Mary just commented on your post." Our brains go something like this: *"Ooh . . . did Mary LIKE what I posted? Or is she being negative AGAIN? Maybe I need to just check real quick before she starts a firestorm on my page. No, I'm going to ignore it for now. This is my Bible study time. Oh heck, I can't concentrate now. I'll just go see*

what she wrote and then come back to my Bible study." Of course, 30 minutes later we realize we got sucked back into social media crap and blew our meditation time. Anyone else??? Airplane mode is your friend! Or at least, turn off all notifications. Seriously . . . it's the only way.

4. ***Don't just pray—meditate.*** What is the difference between prayer and meditation? Well, the simple answer is, praying is when you are *talking* to God. Meditating is when you are *listening* to God. Don't be afraid of silence. Sometimes you can use the friendly timer again for this. Try sitting in silence for one minute. Seriously, just start with ONE MINUTE. Open your heart and mind to whatever God has to say. If your mind wanders, just bring it back to that silent space. It won't be easy at first, but trust me, it gets easier and you'll be able to add another minute and another minute. There are many different meditation apps out there now that you might find helpful as well. The main point is that sitting in silence and giving room for the voice of God to speak is even more important than taking up all the time telling God what you want and need. Truth is, he already knows what you want and need. Allow him some time to enter into the conversation. It may take some time to start hearing from him, but trust me, YOU WILL.

5. ***Journal.*** Use an old fashioned pen and paper to scribble down your thoughts, prayer requests, joys, disappointments, answered prayers, etc. Not only is it therapeutic, but it's also cool to go back and re-read

your words later. You'll be amazed at how God shows up. God tells his people to record his good deeds. Why? Because our memories are incredibly short. How easily we forget God's goodness in our lives. It's been that way throughout history. Just look at how many times God saved the Israelites from certain death, and they were immediately grateful and praised his name. . .only to be grumbling again in no time about how God had surely forgotten them. Writing down all the answered prayers, all the blessings (big and small), all the ways God shows up in our lives, is so very important. Write in those journals, and then every now and then go back and re-read. I know you'll be blown away at how God has shown up in your life time and time again.

Morning routines are meant to be individualized to work for your unique life circumstances, but hopefully these little ideas will give you a place to start because I truly believe it's SO VERY IMPORTANT to start your day in connection with our Creator.

Your Creator.

The One who made you and loves you and desperately wants to be in communion with you. Start your day with God and you'll find a deeper level of connection that lasts throughout your day, giving you hope and peace, no matter what the day might bring.

This is good Soul Care.

Reflections

1. How do you see yourself? As a body or as a soul? How does that affect your over-all sense of self?

2. Do you have a morning routine? How could you add some extra time for spiritual nurturing first thing in the morning?

3. What are a few ways you could implement meditation into your soul care? Maybe you do this later in the day, even in the evening before you go to bed. It's a perfect way to relax your mind and body for a good night's sleep. Set aside a time, find a guide to get started (maybe use an app or a video on YouTube), and give yourself a lot of grace as you begin. Make a plan here:

Soul Care

4. Consider taking a social media break while you get some new spiritual routines in place. Maybe your break is only for a few days or a week. Maybe it's a month. Developing new habits can be hard if you don't allow room/space in your schedule to do so. Most people say that they spend way too much time on social media anyway. How long could you avoid social media? Set a goal here:

5. Have you ever journaled your thoughts? There is something very therapeutic about writing down our feelings and emotions. Almost all therapists encourage this practice as a way of self-reflection. I think it's a great way towards soul-reflection as well. Go buy a beautiful pen and journal to write in. Try it for one month and then go back and re-read your words. I'll bet you will see your own spiritual growth right there in your own words. Write a date to begin this practice here:

CHAPTER THIRTEEN
Abba's Child

"Define yourself radically as one beloved by God…"
—BRENNAN MANNING [1]

THERE ARE MANY NAMES for God in the Bible and I love that they all have unique meanings. Each shows a distinctive side to God's personality. We can use these special names to call upon him in different circumstances. Learning about his biblical names helps us become more intimately acquainted with him. Here are just a few of my favorites:

Elohim—God, our Creator

Jehovah-jireh—God, our Provider

Jehovah-shalom—God of Peace

Jehovah-rapha—God, our Healer

God and My Girlfriends

El Roi—The God who sees

Yahweh—The God of authority

El Shaddai—God, Almighty

Adonai—God, our Master

Elohim Chaseddi—God of Mercy

Abba—God, our Father

In this chapter, I want to focus on the last one. Abba. Our Abba Father, God. We are all his children and he is our Heavenly Father. We can cry out to him for love, comfort and guidance. Just the same as we cry out to earthly fathers for these same things. However, we know that our Godly Father can give us so much more!

Matthew 7:9-11 says:

> ***"Do you know of any parent who would give his hungry child, who asked for food, a plate of rocks instead? Or when asked for a piece of fish, what parent would offer his child a snake instead? If you, imperfect as you are, know how to lovingly take care of your children and give them what's best, how much more ready is your heavenly Father to give wonderful gifts to those who ask him?"*** [2]

Abba's Child

Like I mentioned in the Introduction to this book, some people struggle with using the male term "he" for God. Some especially struggle with picturing him as a "father" figure, and after hearing story after story of women who haven't had good experiences with earthly father figures, I get it.

I am lucky enough to have had the love of several amazing men in my life. My adopted father, my birth father, my husband and my father-in-law have all shown deep and devoted fatherly love to me and our kids. Because of their examples, I've never had a hard time understanding how our Heavenly Father could love us in that beautiful fatherly way. As a little girl, I could run straight into my daddy's arms for comfort and confidence. I always knew I was safe with him. Unfortunately, I've talked with many women who haven't been that lucky. Their earthly fathers didn't set good examples for them to reference. They didn't feel safe with their dads. Some had fathers who abandoned them, or dished out emotional or physical abuse. Their relationship with their fathers was so toxic that even the word "Father" sent a chill up their spine. That just breaks my heart! My prayer for those women is that our Jehova-rapha—Our God, the Healer, would show up in a HUGE way for them and heal the parts of their hearts that were so broken by their earthly fathers, and that they could learn to call out to their ABBA Father and experience true Fatherly love.

Although I majored in music in college, I considered going into psychology for a hot minute. I was always

God and My Girlfriends

fascinated by human behaviors and emotions and how one species could be so varied in almost everything! We all kind of start out the same, as innocent little babies, but then, depending on the nurture we get (or lack of), as well as education and cultural surroundings that we experience, we all become very individual creatures with unique personalities, opinions, wants and needs. However, we all want the love and approval of our parents. No matter how distorted the relationships are, we crave parental love. Many psychological studies actually say that the most important relationship in a female's life is the relationship between her and her father. A positive father-daughter relationship helps shape her self-esteem, her self-image and over-all confidence. It definitely helps shape her opinions of men. Even if we didn't get that support from our earthly fathers, we can STILL get the benefits of a father's love through our Abba Father. HE can help us shape our self-esteem and self-worth. He can help heal how we view ourselves. He reminds us that we are daughters of the King! And you know what? That makes us all Princesses! So we should hold our heads high and remember how valuable we all are.

I made the point earlier that what we think about God is crucial in how we learn to approach God. But how we think about ourselves is equally important in the relationship between God and human beings. If we don't believe that we are truly God's beloved creatures, made in his image, we can get caught up in the lie that we aren't lovable. Satan will try to convince us that we have done too many bad things for God to love us. So even if we DO believe that God is worthy of our love, worship, and admiration, we might still feel like he doesn't really care about us. So why pursue a relationship with him, right? *Wrong.* Believe me, even if we aren't pursuing God, he is *always pursuing us.* God never gives up on us. We are truly his beloved children.

* * *

You Are Not What You Do

Sometimes it can be hard to separate who we are from what we do, or what we have done. I know many women who have confided to me that they feel separated from God because of past mistakes. They feel they have done too much or gone too far for God to still love them. As I shared earlier, I was there myself at one point; however, what I learned is that THAT is the biggest lie from the pit of hell there ever was! We can never go so far away that God can't reach us. Never. And God is *always* reaching out for us! We just have to remember to reach back.

Remember my story in Chapter 11, when I told you how I felt about God after the church refused to let me join their membership? Not only did that whole situation create a distorted view of God for me, but it caused me to form unfair descriptions of myself in my own mind. I decided that I was unlovable, forever scarred and broken from my own actions. I wasn't a good person, so I must be evil. If good, honest, Christian people didn't want me in their midst anymore, then surely their God didn't want me either. It was clear to me that my deeds had created a wall between me and God that was so strong and wide and tall, it would forever be there as a barrier between me and my Creator. Boy, I had really done it, hadn't I?—NOPE. I was wayyyyyy off! Thankfully, I learned that God doesn't work that way, and more importantly, WE don't have that kind of power! There truly is nothing we can do to separate ourselves from the love of God. The apostle Paul tells us this in the book of Romans:

"Do you think anyone is going to be able to drive a wedge between us and Christ's love for us? There is no way! Not trouble, not hard times, not hatred, not hunger, not homelessness, not bullying threats, not backstabbing, not even the worst sins listed in Scripture ... I'm absolutely convinced that nothing—nothing living or dead, angelic or demonic, today or tomorrow, high or low, thinkable or unthinkable—absolutely nothing can get between us and God's love because of the way that Jesus our Master has embraced us."[3]

Once we stop telling ourselves the lie that our past has damaged our ability to be unconditionally loved by God, then we can start believing and understanding that our Abba Father is there for us, loving us, and ready to unite with us. *Always.*

God's love for you is never based on what you have done,

nor is it based on what you are doing now. Many of you are still trying to earn God's love by being "good," and that breaks my heart. I see you out there and I just wanna give you a big hug! You're frantically making sure that you're doing all the things you believe God requires of you, so you can get "into heaven." Look, I get it. I've walked in your shoes. I literally had a checklist of things to do that I felt "covered" me. Some, but not all, are listed below:

Daily Bible Reading — check!

10 minutes or more of prayer time — check!

Tithing 10% — check!

Attending one or more church services that week — check!

Signed up to serve in one or more capacities at church — check!

Pray before meals — check!

Support several ministries — check!

Attend women's bible study — check!

Evangelize to anyone I know that's not a Christian — check!

Pray again at night before I go to sleep — check!

God and My Girlfriends

Friends, you can't do it! You can't earn your way into being loved. You just ARE loved by God! His love stays consistent for us no matter what our actions are that day. He never withdraws his affection for us. You can't do one thing today that is going to make God love you any more or any less than he does right now in this moment! God's love is supernatural and consistent in a way that is hard for us as humans to understand sometimes, because we humans don't have the ability to have that kind of love for one another. Thankfully, God is God, and we are not.

There is a common saying, *"If you don't feel close to God, He's not the one who moved."*

Let that sink in a moment. God doesn't move. God doesn't change. He is the same yesterday, today and tomorrow, and that goes for his love for you as well. He's crazy about you, just exactly as you are. Nothing will ever change that!

You are NOT what you do.

You ARE a daughter of the King.

You are His Beloved. . .So BE-loved.

Rest in that, sweet sisters.

Reflections

1. What is your favorite name of God? How does that name speak to you, personally?

2. How does your relationship with your earthly father affect your ability to relate to God as our Heavenly Father?

3. Was there ever a time you felt like you had gotten "out of favor" with God because of something you did? Think about what made you feel that way. Was it something that *God* did that made you believe that, or was it something a human did or said to you? Or maybe just something you had determined in your own mind?

4. What is one earthly title that you find yourself placing too much of your identity in? For example: wife, mother, helper, daughter, crisis-solver? Maybe it's your job title or another role you fill in life?

5. How would your life/relationships be affected if you started living your life truly believing that you are a Beloved Princess of the King, just as you are right now? Would you make different choices?

CHAPTER FOURTEEN

Evolving Faith

"Doubt is the mechanism by which faith evolves."
—Rachel Held Evans [1]

AS I'VE ALREADY MENTIONED, I grew up as an evangelical Christian. Raised Southern Baptist, then Church of Christ for a few years, before leaving the faith altogether and then returning to what some call a "non-denominational" Christian church. After several years at that church, I found myself back at a Baptist church, this time a Freewill Baptist church. It didn't take long for me to realize I was completely uncomfortable there, so I just stopped going to church altogether for almost six years. When some of my Christian friends hear me say that, they almost always make a sad face and say something like, "Ohhhhh . . . I'm so sorry that happened." But then when I tell them that I'm not sorry at all because those six years were some of the best spiritual years of my life, they look confused. How can that be? Well, because for the first time

God and My Girlfriends

EVER in my life, I dug into my Bible on my own and did the deepest true Bible study I had ever done. I asked the Holy Spirit to be my teacher instead of only relying on interpretations of the leadership of any particular church.

It was during this time I became acquainted with Rachel Held Evans. I say "acquainted" with her but that's a little misleading. I felt I somehow knew her because I followed her on twitter—LOL. So, although I was "acquainted" with *her*, she wasn't actually acquainted with *me*. I remember hearing her name being whispered about in my previous religious circles, but it was only used in those hushed tones that you use when talking about someone who had "lost their way." So I steered clear for a while. However, after leaving the church and deciding that it was time for me and the Holy Spirit to hash out my spiritual situation, once and for all, I was led once again to Rachel. The first book I read of hers was originally titled *Evolving in Monkey Town* and it rocked my world . . . in a good way! *Evolving in Monkey Town* has now been re-issued with a new title. It is now called *Faith Unraveled* and while that IS probably a clearer description of what the book is about, I'm still kind of partial to the original title.

Rachel lived in the small, Tennessee town of Dayton, where the famous Scopes Monkey Trial took place in 1925. This was the legal case formally called "The State of Tennessee vs. John Thomas Scopes." John T. Scopes was a high school teacher who was arrested and tried for violating the Tennessee Butler's Act, which made it unlawful to

Evolving Faith

teach human evolution in any state-funded school. The trial drew intense national attention. Famous lawyers were brought in to handle both sides of the case, and reporters from all over the country set up camp outside the courthouse. The atmosphere quickly turned into more of a circus than a trial.

I won't bore you with more details of the trial (if you are interested, just google "Scopes Monkey Trial"—or watch the classic movie *Inherit The Wind*), but let me just say that it became way more about "religion vs science" than about this one high school teacher. It basically set up the Modernists against the Fundamentalists, which is something that is still going on today in both political and religious settings.

Apparently, Dayton is still a very conservative area with fundamentalism at the forefront of the culture. That sets the backdrop for Rachel's upbringing, even steering her to a fundamentalist university for advanced learning. However, along the way, she started having questions. Questions that no one seemed to have answers to. That's what started her journey of evolving faith.

Reading Rachel's book was the encouragement I needed to pursue my own evolving spiritual journey. Her story mirrored my own childhood and young adult experiences. My heart almost leapt with joy at the kinship I felt towards her, though I hadn't even met her. Someone understands me!!! YES! I immediately found her on twitter and it was awesome to see her sharp mind (and wit) wrangle tough conversations and stand firm on issues that she believed in. This woman had clearly done her research and she always had biblical back-up, even as some people called her a heretic when she didn't agree with their theology.

I paid close attention as she and her friend Sarah Bessey started The Evolving Faith Conference in 2018. I wanted so badly to attend, but I couldn't because of my own crazy touring schedule that year. I had a few other friends who attended and told me how amazing it was. I decided right then and there that I would go to the 2019 conference and hopefully, finally meet Rachel in person. I also hoped to get more acquainted with other leaders that had helped me come back to my faith. Leaders like Peter Enns, Barbara Brown-Taylor, Osheta Moore, Jeff Chu and of course, Sarah Bessey.

On April 14, 2019, I remember Rachel posting a tweet, asking for prayers as she was struggling with a bad bout of the flu. She even joked about having to miss *Game Of Thrones* because she was now in the hospital after a bad reaction to the medicine they gave her. That was her last tweet. Rachel passed away on May 4th, 2019. I just couldn't believe that she was gone and that her voice, so desperately needed by so many was silenced. I had never even met this woman and I deeply grieved. I grieved for her husband, Dan and their two little babies. I grieved for the rest of her family and close friends. I grieved for

Evolving Faith

all of the Evolving Faith community who had lost one of their champions. And I grieved for me. . .and it was weird. I've never grieved so much for someone I had never even met. However, the Holy Spirit reminded me once again that I wasn't supposed to rely on any one human to be my spiritual advisor. That was the Holy Spirit's job. He is the one who helps my faith "evolve" and that is *truth*.

I still miss Rachel, but I'm grateful that she introduced me to a whole new community of like-minded believers. I recently found *The Evolving Faith Podcast* and the very first episode was "Remembering Rachel Held Evans." They played her entire speech from that first EF Conference in North Carolina, and it was an awesome and inspiring message. One topic she addressed was: "What does it really mean to say your faith is *"evolving"?"* It doesn't mean that your faith is more evolved than others. It doesn't mean that it's more spiritual, more enlightened, or better than. It simply means that your faith is moving and changing and adapting so that it can survive. My faith was dying a slow death under past theological teachings. I needed to have someone help me find a way to hang on to my love of Jesus and the Bible, because I was just about to walk away from it all. . .but then came RHE. I'll be forever grateful. She put in the hard work so that others like me could find their way back to God. She was a flashlight on the darkened path for us. I could hear her voice saying, "It's okay out here in the wilderness. We aren't lost. There are a lot of us out here. We are all helping each other find our spiritual eyes and ears so that we can see and hear God more clearly." Just to clarify, that isn't an actual quote from Rachel, but it's what I imagined her saying and it was so very comforting.

Rachel was one of the first to help point me back to a religion that I loved. To help me see it with fresh eyes. To understand that it was okay to have doubts and questions, and that God is so much bigger than the God of my youth. I'm not saying I have it all figured out, or that I ever will, but I do know that I now have a deeper connection with Jesus, and I'm grateful for the ability to embrace mystery in my spiritual journey. There have been many others who have influenced me since I found her writings —teachers, pastors, spiritual advisors and friends. Some who I know personally and others who I do not but hope to meet someday.

* * *

Faith vs. Religion

RELIGION: The main thing I have learned throughout my spiritual journey is that there is a big difference between *faith* and religion. One of my favorite quotes from Father Richard Rohr is:

> *"Religions should be understood as only the fingers that points us to the moon, but not the moon itself."* [2]

Evolving Faith

For many years, I put my faith in my religion, not God. I thought that my religion could save me. I thought that having the right belief system was the way to get to God. Now I believe differently. Now I see that it's not a correct set of beliefs that will connect me with my Creator. No, a correct set of beliefs is not the same as a cultivated, reliant relationship. And *that*, my friends, is what we ultimately want. We want a relationship with our Creator—our God who loves us so deeply.

Now, I'm not discounting religion or religious practices. Like Father Rohr says, they can help "point us to the moon." I just want to offer encouragement here to make sure you are prioritizing a connection with God over a connection with religion. I practice the religion of Christianity, so my way to God is through Jesus Christ and the Holy Spirit, but others may find God through different religions. Part of my own faith evolution and journey is to no longer discount other religions. Jesus says in John 10:16, *"I have sheep not of this fold."* I feel it would be arrogant of me to think that God isn't big enough to have ways of revealing himself to *all*, ways that I'm not capable of understanding. I know that many of my more conservative-based Christian friends might be gasping at that right now and will be tempted to call or text me with many a bible verse that will "prove" to me that Christianity is the only way, but getting into that kind of debate is not what this book is for or about. That kind of discussion is best done in person over a strong cup of coffee. Or maybe that will be my next book. ;-) My point is only that religion is one thing, faith is another.

So . . . what is faith?

FAITH: There are two different definitions of the word "faith" in the dictionary:

1. Complete trust or confidence in something or someone.

2. A strong belief in God, based on spiritual understanding, rather than proof.

And if we go to the Bible, we find another definition:

> ***"Now faith is confidence in what we hope for and assurance about what we do not see. . . ."*** [3]

What do we learn about faith from those three definitions? Well, first off . . . faith is *not* a belief system. It isn't based on proof either. Faith is confidence in something unseen, unproven. And faith is definitely *not* certainty, which is a relief to someone like me who struggles so much with doubt.

> *"The opposite of faith is not doubt, but certainty. Certainty is missing the point entirely."*
> —ANNE LAMOTT [4]

Well, BOOM. If that ain't the truth! If we can prove

Evolving Faith

with absolute certainty that something is real, then we negate the whole "faith" thing entirely, don't we? I'm not kidding when I say Anne's quote is a truth I rely on constantly. Doubts can plague me almost daily, which used to make me think my faith was weak. What I have learned in the last few years is that it's my doubts that have brought me closer to God and deepened my faith. It's my doubts that have caused me to dig deeper into Bible study, spend more time in prayer, and (ultimately) "keep the faith."

Another great quote is from the book *The Sin of Certainty*, by author Pete Enns. He states:

> ***"The life of Christian faith is more than agreeing with a set of beliefs about Christ, morality, or how to read the Bible. It means being so intimately connected to Christ that his crucifixion is ours, his death is our death, and his life is our life—which is hardly something we can grasp with our minds. It has to be experienced. It is an experience."*** [5]

I love that last line—faith IS an experience. It's my experience. It's your experience. Each one of us has the opportunity to have our own unique relationship with God. It is my desire that every single person reading this can find their own way to that deep connection. It truly is the greatest gift of life on earth.

Reflections

1. What does the phrase "evolving faith" mean to you? Does it make you uncomfortable? Maybe even scare you a bit? Why?

2. Have you ever found yourself attaching a large part of your identity in your religious affiliation? How has it affected your life—good or bad?

3. There is a difference between faith and religion. How can those two go hand-in-hand?

4. How does your current religion increase your faith?

5. What is one way you can let go of the need for certainty? How would this affect your faith?

CHAPTER FIFTEEN

Rooted In The Eternal

"I pray that you may have your roots and foundation in love. . ."
—Ephesians 3:17[1]

THE COVID-19 PANDEMIC hit America hard in March 2020. I'll never forget the day I was on the phone with my son as he warned me that what we were about to experience was going to be a long-term situation, but I was still in a bit of disbelief. I said to my oldest boy, *"Derek, I'm heading to Costco today to get groceries for a good two weeks, because we may have to quarantine in our homes that long. Do you want to go with me?"* There was a long pause on the other end of the phone line, and then Derek calmly and sweetly said, *"Mom, I think you are severely underestimating what we are about to face with this virus. We don't need to prepare for an event. We need to prepare for a season. This isn't a hurricane coming. This is winter."* Boy . . . was he ever right! I just couldn't grasp what we were all about to face for the rest of 2020 and beyond. We were about to have a complete breakdown of everything familiar and secure in a way I had never seen in my lifetime. It was the moment everything changed for us, not only in America, but all over the world.

* * *

Staying Connected

One of the things that dramatically changed that March of 2020 was the way we all did "church." I was particularly bummed because at that time, I had only recently started attending a church on a regular basis, after not having a church home for many years. It felt so good to have consistent fellowship with like-minded believers again and now, because of the virus, it seemed it was all coming to a screeching halt. I have always had a love-hate relationship with technology, but during this time I was SO grateful for it, as it allowed our church and most other churches in the country to continue to meet together online. Not only did our church offer a service every Sunday morning that I could attend from the comfort of my couch and PJs (I know you guys watched church in your pajamas too so don't even try to tell me you didn't!)—but I also was blessed to have a wonderful women's group that met on Zoom every Sunday morning. These women were a lifeline and Godsend to me during that crucial time in my faith journey, and I'll forever be grateful for them. Zoom helped us all stay connected at a time when I think we were all desperately needing connection. Technology can get a bad rap at times, but in situations like this, it can definitely be a blessing.

One particular Sunday morning in Sept of 2020, I was feeling extra raw about the state of our world and our country. I really didn't feel like gathering in community and was leaning towards staying in bed with my head under the covers. But, at the last minute, I put on my robe and grabbed a cup of coffee and opened my Zoom link to join the ladies for our Sunday morning group and BOY HOWDY, God gave me a WORD that morning that I desperately needed. I believe God has many different ways that he speaks to us, and one of the most common ways I find that God speaks is through my friends. He used my friend, Tammy Starling, to speak to me in a very loud and dramatic way that Sunday morning. (Just to clarify, sweet Tammy isn't loud and dramatic. She is actually one of the kindest and most soft-spoken women I've ever met. But she speaks such truth that even if she were to whisper it, it can feel like a brick of truth right to your forehead!) I honestly don't even know exactly what we were discussing that morning. I was there kind of half-hearted and disconnected, and I had probably only had a couple of sips of coffee. . .but I remember Tammy's words loud and clear.

*"The only way we can withstand all that the world is throwing at us right now is by staying connected to the Vine. We must stay **rooted in the eternal.**"*

Those words jumped out at me like an arrow being shot right in my heart. It was as if God turned up the volume extra loud when she said it and it felt like a Spiritual 2x4 hitting me square upside the head! It was like God was saying "PAY ATTENTION WOMAN!!" So I did. I tucked those words into my heart and started praying over those words daily.

A few days later, I was listening to a podcast, and I suddenly heard the words *"stay rooted"* again. They jumped out in a sentence and I was like, "Whoa! There are those words again." Later in the week, I was watching a video -- and GUESS WHAT WORDS JUMPED OUT AT ME??? Yep. For a third time in just a few days, I heard the words *"stay rooted"* in a sentence. It was as if God was just making *sure* I got the message.

I believe that this is one of the many ways that God chooses to communicate with us - when we get repeated messages from different sources. We must keep our spiritual eyes and ears open in order to recognize these little messages from God. This particular message of "staying rooted" reminds me of one of my favorite scriptures:

> *"I am The Vine and you are the branches. If you remain in me and I in you, you will bear much fruit. Apart from me, you can do nothing."* —JOHN 15:5 [2]

Ya'll, the world is gonna throw some crazy hard stuff at all of us, and it will be our connections to God and to each other that will carry us through. Life isn't meant to be done alone, and even on those days when we might feel abandoned by humans, God is always there. *Always.* I've had too many dark nights alone with only God to get me through to NOT believe that truth.

Our time on this earth is fleeting. We need to choose how we spend our time wisely. We can gather up a million riches, spend hours at the gym getting the perfect physique, work ourselves to death people pleasing. . .and for what? In the end, will any of that really matter? What I believe truly matters is the work we do that will impact our souls and the souls of those around us—preparing us for the next life. For our *eternal* home. The only way to do that is to stay rooted in what matters to God. Rooted in Christ. Rooted in love. Rooted in the eternal.

This is why I started *God and My Girlfriends Ministries* a few years ago, because I saw too many amazing women around me focusing on things that didn't matter, and forgetting how special they were to God; because I wanted to give them encouragement and real tools to enhance the relationships in their lives; because I wanted them to learn how to love and BE LOVED well.

I hope this book might be one of those tools for you. I hope you'll find inspiration to nurture these important relationships in your life. And I hope you'll feel more confident to live in the beauty of relationship—relationship with God, your girlfriends. . .and you.

Reflections

1. What does the word "rooted" mean to you?

2. Commit to memory John 15:5. It helps me to write down things I'm trying to memorize. Write it here:

3. How does it make you feel to know that we have a power much greater than our own that we can stay connected to every moment of every day?

4. What does "the eternal" mean to you? Is it scary or comforting to you to think of another realm that our souls will experience? Why?

5. How can our continued focus on God, our Creator, help us to be better for ourselves and others?

Epilogue

REMEMBER MY FRIEND, Laura?

"What do you mean, exactly?" I gently asked. *"Do you think you need to see a doctor?"* I heard her sigh deeply and then she said, *"I don't know. Maybe. All I know is that I can't go on like this for one more day."* It was at that moment I said, *"I'm getting in my car right now. I'll be at your house in 10 mins. DON'T GO ANYWHERE."*

When she opened the door to her home, I could tell she was beyond "tired". . .

Yes, she was tired, spent, exhausted. . .I saw it all over her face when she opened her door. But as I looked into her eyes, I saw something else in that moment: *A SPARK OF HOPE*. It was dim, but yes, there it was. I saw *hope* when she saw me standing there in her doorway.

God and My Girlfriends

Did that hope come from thinking that I had all the answers and was going to immediately offer her relief from her problems? No, it wasn't that at all. There is a hope that comes with community—when we realize we aren't going to have to face our problems alone. THAT'S the hope I saw in her when she saw me standing at her door. Now she knew that she had a friend to help carry her burdens and walk beside her towards a better place.

I've certainly been there before, when I've been carrying a load too heavy, or a secret too dark, or a burden too great. Having a friend show up and say, "Sister, we will get through this together"—*that* is what relationship is all about. It's what God wants for us, doing life together as fragile, messed-up, sometimes crazy human beings!

Girlfriends, let's show up for one another. Let's fight for each other. Let's remember that we really do have the ability to add so much love into the lives of those that God places around us.

I pray this book will be a blessing to you. I hope you will read it together—in community. Use the reflections to grow and encourage one another. Keep working towards better understandings of each other, yourselves, and of God. Spread this message of hope, community, acceptance and love everywhere you go. That's how we can make this world a better place.

No more carrying burdens alone.

Epilogue

We are in this together, sisters.

God bless us all.

Acknowledgments

This book would have never been possible without the help from these wonderful people:

My love, Mike Waldron: Your support and encouragement is unrivaled in my life. You truly make me better at everything I do and I'm so grateful God brought us together. You are not only an amazing husband, father and grandfather — but you are my very best friend. You have my heart forever.

Our kids, Derek, Kari and Sam: You three wonderful humans make me proud every single day. Thanks for always supporting me and believing in me. I love you all.

Emily Wells: You're a wonderful wife, an amazing daughter-in-law and incredible mother to Charlotte and Oliver. Your support with *God and My Girlfriends Ministries,* as well as with this book has meant the world to me. Thanks for the hours of editing and proof-reading. I owe ya, BIG! Love you!

Mary Sue Englund: Your dedication to helping me get this book out in the world was amazing! From your beautiful cover art to the hours of formatting—your fingerprints are all over this one and I'm SO grateful for your gifts and for your friendship. Thank you, thank you, my friend!

Mark Smeby: Thank you for the endless encouragement and tangible support with this book and GAMG ministries. You are a treasure to me!

Lori Roberts: thank you for sharing your time and expertise to make this book so much better. On the next "Sister trip", drinks are on me! Love you!

My mastermind gals: Stacey Wynn and Marie Griffith. I'm so very grateful for all you do to help me and GAMG Ministries grow. Glad I have this sisterhood!

Along the process of writing this book, several of my friends and family have been specifically supportive in different ways to help keep me on track and get this book finished. I appreciate you all so much!

A big THANK YOU to: *Lisa Hancock, Britt Savage, Kim Parent, Juli Hood, Melissa Irwin, Carole Ford, Vanessa Connor, Sherree Telford, Todd and Terri Woolsey, Stephcynie Curry, Jewelee Peters, Sonia Lee, Sara Light,*

Acknowledgments

Rob and Lara Harris, Melissa Jackson, Marla Richardson, Donna Ruffin, Ramona McKenzie, Katarina Bibova, and Valerie Howerton.

And finally, thanks to ***Ron and Jan Waldron, Raul and Marina Zamora,*** and ***Valorie Wise-Jones.*** Mike and I are both so grateful to have loving parents who guide us and love us well. We are blessed by you more than you could ever know.

*Special acknowledgement: Manuel and Betty Ramirez — Mom & Dad, you left this earth too soon to be part of this process, but your influence is the thread that holds it together. Love, always.

Notes

INTRODUCTION:
1. Matthew 22:36-40 - The Bible (NIV)
2. Common quote from Deepok Chopra
3. Common quote from Richard Rohr
4. 1 Corinthians 13:1 - The Bible (NIV)
5. John 4:24 and Genesis 1:27

PART ONE:
1. Quote by Audre Lorde -(From the 1988 book, "A Burst of Light: And Other Essays")

CHAPTER 1:
1. Common quote by Henry Ford, American business magnate (unknown origin)
2. Common quote by Maya Angelou, poet, actress, activist (unknown origin)
3. Philippians 4:8 (NIV) - The Holy Bible
4. Common quote by Priscilla Shirer (unknown origin)

CHAPTER 2:
1. Quote by Katie Reed, via "The Borderline Blog" w/Katie Reed: www.katiereed.com

CHAPTER 3:
1. Quote by Steven Pinker, cognitive psychologist, linguist, and popular science author (unknown origin)
2. Quote by Lysa TerKeurst, from her book, "The Best Yes"

CHAPTER 4:
1. Ecclesiastes 3:1 - The Holy Bible
2. David Moses Perez, lead pastor at Spero Dei Church in Nashville, TN

CHAPTER 5:
1. Quote by Brené Brown, author, speaker and research professor - from her book "The Gifts of Imperfection"
2. Psalm 39: 13 - 16, The Msg translation, The Holy Bible
3. Thoughts from Max Lucado's book, "Cure For The Common Life"
4. Direct quote from Max Lucado's book, "Cure For The Common Life"

God and My Girlfriends

PART TWO: Proverbs 27:9—The Holy Bible

CHAPTER 6:
1. Quote from Deron Spoo, minister and author - from his book "The Good Book"
2. Genesis 2:18 - The Holy Bible
3. From the Forbes.com article, "Millennials and the Loneliness Epidemic" by Neil Howe, May 3rd, 2019
4. Source: https://www.wbur.org/onpoint/2020/03/23/vivek-murthy-loneliness

CHAPTER 7:
1. Common quote from Martin Luther King, minister and peace activist- (unknown origin)
2. Quote from "Braving The Wilderness" by Brené Brown
3. Common quote by Maya Angelo—(unknown origin)
4. Common quote by Maya Angelo—(unknown origin)

CHAPTER 8:
1. Quote from William Sloane Coffin Jr., minister and peace activist -(unknown origin)
2. "It Takes All Kinds of Kinds" written by Don Henry and Phillip Coleman, recorded by Miranda Lambert
3. Based on the book, "Unorthodox: The Scandalous Rejection of My Hasidic Roots" by Deborah Feldman
4. Sign origins: https://www.welcomeyourneighbors.org/

CHAPTER 9:
1. Public quote from William James, American philosopher and psychologist (unknown origin)
2. "You can't make old friends"—written by Ryan Hannah King, Don Schlitz, and Caitlyn Smith
3. Quote by Mike Waldron

CHAPTER 10:
1. Proverbs 17:17 - The Holy Bible
2. 1 Samuel 18:1 - The Holy Bible
3. 2 Timothy 4:11 - The Holy Bible
4. Proverbs 27:9 - NLT - The Holy Bible
5. Quote by author and poet C.J. Heck

Notes

PART THREE: Luke 1:45 - The Holy Bible

CHAPTER 11:
1. Quote from AZ Tozer, American Christian pastor, author - from his book, "The Knowledge of the Holy"
2. Quote from a tweet from author, speaker and minister, Beth Moore on April 15th, 2019

CHAPTER 12:
1. Quote from John Ortberg, Christian author, speaker, pastor - from his book, "Soul Keeping"
2. Matthew 6:33 - The Holy Bible, The Message translation
3. Quote from Kathie Lee Gifford, tv personality, singer, songwriter, author—from her book, "The Rock, The Road and The Rabbi"

CHAPTER 13:
1. Quote from Brennan Manning, author, priest, speaker - from his book, "Abba's Child"
2. Matthew 7:9-11, The Holy Bible, The Passion translation
3. Romans 8: 35 -39, The Holy Bible, The Message translation

CHAPTER 14:
1. Quote from Rachel Held Evans, blogger, speaker, author - from her book, "Faith Unraveled" (previously titled, "Evolving In Monkey Town")
2. Common quote by Father Richard Rohr
3. Hebrews 11:1, The Holy Bible—NIV translation
4. Anne Lamott quote, originally credited to "Father Tom"
5. Peter Enns, from his book "The Sin Of Certainty"

CHAPTER 15:
1. Ephesians 3:17, The Holy Bible, GNT translation
2. John 15:5, The Holy Bible, NIV translation